The MAN whose EYES are OPEN

Oluwafemi O. Emmanuel

Copyright © 2016. All rights reserved.

No part of this publication may be reproduced, stored in a retrieval system or transmitted in any way by any means, electronic, mechanical, photocopy, recording or otherwise, without the prior permission of the author except as provided by USA copyright law.

All characters appearing in this work are fictitious. Any resemblance to real persons, living or dead, is purely coincidental.

The opinions expressed by the author are not necessarily those of Revival Waves of Glory Books & Publishing.

Published by Revival Waves of Glory Books & Publishing

PO Box 596| Litchfield, Illinois 62056 USA

www.revivalwavesofgloryministries.com

Revival Waves of Glory Books & Publishing is committed to excellence in the publishing industry.

Book design Copyright © 2016 by Revival Waves of Glory Books & Publishing. All rights reserved.

Published in the United States of America

ISBN 978-1684111787

Oluwafemi O. Emmanuel

Dedication

This book is dedicated to every child of God who is endlessly seeking for a revival.

Contents

Dedication iii

Preface v

Chapter 1: BLESSINGS FOR THE ELECT 1

Chapter 2: THE ENEMIES AND YOU 7

Chapter 3: WHAT YOU CHOOSE TO SEE............................ 18

Chapter 4: THE REVELATION OF GOD
                   IN THE SPIRITUAL BATTLE............................ 27

Chapter 5: SEEING THE POTENTIAL..................................... 47

chapter 6: SEEING FROM GOD'S
                   ANGLE (Mystery in God's Will)......................... 63

Chapter 7: SEEING VANITY 73

Chapter 8: BLINDNESS AND SPIRITUAL CATARACT 82

Chapter 9: SEEING GOD 90

Chapter 10: OPEN EYES: A MUST IN THIS AGE 108

About the author... 120

About the Book 121

Preface

Hosea 4:6 says, "My people perish because they lack knowledge…" In this world, for every person, ignorant is not an excuse especially for Christians. The children of this world are never tired of hunting down anyone for their progress, and Satan, their father, never rests in his operations against the people of God. But we the children of the living God cannot afford to allow them; we must be wiser than them. That is why we must get our spiritual sense organ in alert; we must get our spiritual eyes opened.

Getting our eyes opened is as saying, "In all thy getting's, get understanding"; it is like the heart of the prudence getting knowledge, and not far behind the situation going on in his environment, but he is very much aware of any matter that may arise; either in a gradual process or rapidly which may be causing any effect whatsoever. And by that he may know the correct application to anticipate the issue. That is, when we understand everything that has to do with our journey through this world as a Christian; we will know the right application fit into every situations of life.

The Bible says that the eyes is the light of the body, then that means without it we are in darkness, we fall into any trap, ditch, or hit ourselves against anything, dash our foot against the stone, and so on. It is not a good thing for a person without the physical eyes, but it is worse for a person to be without the spiritual eyes, even as a Christian. The fact is, we can live our lives a little comfortably without our physical eyes, but as a Christian anyone who lacks the spiritual eyes or whose spiritual eyes is not open is very much prone to calamity, and can make to be a victim of spiritual theft or robbery; it can cause a digression in a journey of destiny, and it can make one to be susceptible to every Satanic attacks.

Many Christians suffer today because they lack spiritual eyes. Many churches today suffers the attack of Satan because their spiritual eyes are not open, and so many people in the world today are very much blinded to conspiracies of principalities and powers, and rulers of darkness of this world.

In this book, we shall discuss extensively about the advantages of an opening eye, the will of God for it, and what could blind us. And I pray as we journey through the book, every eye shall be open in Jesus name.

Chapter 1

BLESSINGS FOR THE ELECT

Numbers 23 vs. 9-10 says, *"For from the top of the rocks I see him and from the hills I behold him: lo, the people shall not be reckoned among the nations. Who can count the dust of Jacob, and the number of the fourth part of Israel? Let me die the death of the righteous, and let my last end be like this..."*

The reference above is a portion for every believer; every believer needs to claim and enjoy the benefit God has promised. The thought of God is to give us what will generate peace into our lives, that is we the chosen ones; a blessed inheritance has being programmed for us in this world, and in the world to come which is eternal. We are not meant to lack good things since God is our shepherd to supply all our needs, we are not to be troubled since Christ has overcome the world, and we are not to be confused since the Holy Spirit is our guide.

According to the Bible, those the Lord has chosen to believe in Him were incredibly blessed. Abraham was blessed after he was called by God out from his pagan family. God made a covenant with him to bring out from him a nation of which two came out to be.

The Man Whose Eyes Are Open

Abraham was passing through Canaan land when God promised him the land as an inheritance to his descendants of which it eventually came to pass after hundreds of years. And as Isaac who was the promised child shared in his father's blessings, so also his son, Jacob, who was chosen by God from the womb and Esau his brother also continued in the blessing. David stood out to be chosen to have an uncommon faith in God to do beyond imagination even as a little boy, and being an adult he was greatly blessed and was also given an everlasting covenant of blessing.

Their lives established the truth about the lives of we the believers today that we are also chosen out of the multitude in the world by the grace of God unto Him and through the exercises of our faith in God we are automatically entitled to some great benefits: salvation, miracle, success, riches, divine inheritance, authority and so on. But there is something that Is common in the lives of these people we have mentioned; that need to be thoroughly studied and be adopted, that is, how they have carefully followed through the mandate of God and His directions, how they have exercised their faith in obedience. They were patient, attentive and diligent before God in bringing to pass God's promises.

Israel was not chosen by accident. It was arranged by God to demonstrate His power and to sanctify His name amongst the nations. The Bible reveals in Numbers 24 that it pleases God to bless Israel (the Lord's chosen race). Israel, as a nation, was particularly separated from every other nation in the world (1 Kings 8 vs 53) to be sanctified for Him only and so they were meant to be blessed.

And because of that, the Lord needed them to be like their forefathers in how they have carefully followed Him. He needed their full attention; the Bible says in Deut. 30 vs 8-9 "...*And thou shall return and obey the voice of the LORD, and do all his commandments which I command thee this day. And in the fruit of thy cattle, and thy God will make thee plenteous in every work of thine hand, in the fruit of thy body, and in the fruit of thy cattle, and in the fruit of thy land, for the Lord will again rejoice over thee for good, as he rejoiced over thy fathers"*. That is for God to rejoice over someone then that person must have pleased Him to a certain degree. And also in Prov. 22 vs 28, *"Remove not the ancient landmark, which thy fathers have set"*. Like their fathers, God needed them to have faith in Him, to obey Him, to receive from Him always that they may be able to perceive what God have in mind for them as He has promised them. Even though the Lord has chosen Israel to demonstrate His power, He has satisfied them with victory and with some miraculous sightings; the parting sea, angelic foods, water from the rock and even made them to hear His great awesome voice, and yet they lost their inner sight of the awesomeness of Jehovah God. That the Israelites may observe God well He provided them the cloud on the tabernacle by day and the pillar of fire by night as a guidance for their movement. But the Israelites refused to understand; they were double minded, despite clues and sign, warnings and admonitions yet they were unable to foresee even the promises of their portion as the chosen nation. But those whose faith is strong, those who diligently observed God so well were singled out of their generation to witness the fulfillment of God's promises (Heb. 3 vs 16-19).

Galatians 3 vs 29 says *"And if ye be Christ's, then are ye Abraham's seed, and heirs according to the promise."*

As Abraham was called and chosen out from the world so also we Christians are called out from the world. And as the children of Israel was freed from the bondage of the Egyptians to worship God, so also we the church of God was called out from the bondage of Satan to worship Him. And for every believer there is a promise of blessing in this world and in the world to come. God has given us His Word for our learning, the Holy Spirit for our guidance that we may not fall to the error of those who rebel against God, and most of all to see clearly the inheritance of God for our lives and to have hope (Rom. 15:4, 2 Tim. 3:16).

Stick to the Promise as Pronounced and No Impromptu

God is never too late in fulfilling His promises, even though it may seems He tarries. But He had said in His word and is still saying it, that none of His words will go unfulfilled; what He will do today He will not postponed it till tomorrow. Waiting on the Lord's promises will yield great reward but not waiting puts one into trouble. Remember the mistake of Abram and Sarai when God told them that they will surely have a son who will be the real heir yet they lost their sight on the promise and created an impromptu arrangement to the promise.

Even though Sarai concluded that God had refused to give her a child, eventually God in His faithfulness fulfilled His promise, but their mistake had become a calamity to them already. Sarai was strongly paranoid on the behaviour of Hagar towards her and put the blame on Abram instead of admitting to the fact that she made a terrible mistake by simply involving Hagar into her marriage because of her unbelief, and ask for forgiveness from God and from her husband But the frustration turned her to be harsh and seemed wicked; igniting the fire of anger within her. I believe Hagar will not be the only person who will suffer from her wrath at that very moment, she may even disregard and be also harsh against any other handmaid at that very moment and no one would have gained her favour.

If we read chapter sixteen of the book of Genesis, we will see that Hagar found favour from God. God warned her to be more submissive to Sarai no matter how justified she may think she was because she may be thinking she had almost equal right with Sarai since she had the first son [for that matter] for Abram.

And then in chapter 21, even though Sarah was only paranoid about Hagar's behaviour, this time she saw Ishmael's mockery, and for the fact that Abraham loved his son, grievance arouse between him and Sarah. And eventually without God's will, Abraham had to send Hagar and Ishmael away giving them only bread and a bottle of water which seems cruel. Now, how can Ishmael and Hagar forget being mistreated by Mr. and Mrs. Abraham? But God was always there to assist Hagar, as our God is impartial. But we all know the atrocities the people of the Bond Woman are causing now. Up till today the fight still goes on. Their Empires and those that follow them have never been with peace with the children of the promise and the heirs of Abraham through Christ Jesus.

My point is losing sight on the promises of God is a dangerous thing and this is a great sin of unbelief, and those that are involved ended up in a ditch. Many people have compromised because they lost hope; because they cannot wait on the Lord. A brother came to me and said it seems that his prayers are not answered. So, I asked him what can he say about prayer. When he was unable to give me a point, I said, "Prayer can be said to be 'waiting upon God'", and I enlightened him with some instances in the Bible. My point is when you pray, believe God is hearing you and then the waiting will be your persistence prayer and faith. God is not a man.

"God is not a man, that He should lie; neither the son of man, that He should repent: hath He said, and shall He not do it? or hath He spoken and shall He not make it good?"

Numbers 23 vs 19.

Chapter 2

THE ENEMIES AND YOU

In every Christian's journey, we are expected by God to fulfill our destiny; not how far but how well we live our lives. But in every journey there is usually an obstruction; the enemy of the destiny, a diversion on the highway which brings frustration, temptation, fear, and doubt unexpectedly most of the time when we are not ready. We are liable to have a set-back or shortcomings if we are not careful. But to be able to reach our goal in life, our eyes must really see every forthcomings, and we have to look beyond it.

As we acknowledge that there are enemies of progress, let us also understand that in them are strategies we cannot afford to underestimate. For example, Israel did not think that there would be a great perception about them from elsewhere, neither did they think that there will be another strategy to attack them besides waging a physical war. But there comes a man who has perceived God's people's future, a man who is not an Israelite but an ally to the enemy, a soothsayer of the highest order, a man of a great gift but who will rather use it for his own selfish gain: I introduce to you Balaam, the son of Boer of Pethor.

There are things to learn as a Christian in the case of Balak, Balaam and the Israelites in Numbers. 22, 23, 24, and 25.

I. The truth is that our enemies knew us since the day we were born-again, since the day we were redeemed and set free by Christ from the bondage of Satan to be God's children. And they are aware of your increase both spiritually and physically of which they see as a hindrance and as a potential loss to them. Remember in chapter 22 vs 5, Balak sent a message to Balaam saying, *"Behold, there is a people come out of Egypt* (that is out of the bondage of sin) *they cover the face of the earth,* (spiritual increment aiding the physical blessing) *and they abide over against me* (that is looking like a potential threat to him)". Of course the alarm of your previous victory has been sounded across their territory; that victory you thought it was just normal, that achievements you thought was common, is a great disturbance to the enemies, they knew you are the son of the most high God and you can hinder their movement in your life and in the life of others.

II. There are consults concerning your life as a child of God. Remember the Bible says the people of Moab meet with the elders of Midian (in Num. 22 vs 4) to discuss about the people — Israel. Which equally means that there is a counsel of high order against you as a Christian; they are sitting at the table in the dark, setting strategies on marks, and they are those who the Bible talks about in Psalm 2 vs 1-3? They don't want you to be in control of them but rather tyrannize your life. They offer rewards to the detriment of your life. And besides the dark counsel, if God almighty shows you the thoughts of those who you think love you; your relatives and friends and so on, you will be surprised. As it has been mostly acknowledged in a race, the first and the second are enemies to themselves because the second will want to see the first to fail but unto his own advantage.

III. Our enemies are futurist. They can have the perception of what you are capable of, as the prophet can foresee your greatness so also the devil can have the foreknowledge of your strength. And obviously through the investigation on your past victories your future is being understood. They perceive beyond your own perception about your future. They imagine beyond your imagination, and so they anticipate beyond your expectation.

IV. And finally, if one is not careful they can detect your key. They will keep on coming and banging on the door till it opens unless one is heavily shielded.

And now, brethren it is dangerous for us if we cannot describe our future; the kind of marriage we want, the kind of ministry God has given us or the kind of career God as programmed for you, etc. We need to try and perceive more than the enemies. We need to be wiser than them through the commandments of

God. If the Israelites knew these four lessons, I believe strongly that chapter 25 of the book of Numbers wouldn't have been a record of their woe. We the children of God cannot afford to fall behind the enemy concerning our destiny; we cannot afford to let them see beyond our sight. Let's pray to God that we may see beyond our enemies that we may boycott their plans against our lives.

Balaam

In the Old Testament, Balaam is a man with high recognition. He is mostly known for his occupation from Mesopotamia to the Mediterranean, and throughout the Canaanite lands as a prominent and feared sorcerer, a forecaster, a prophet and a soothsayer and he is very good in his works. He was a man with a powerful gift of prophesy, and may have been a prophet for God almighty initially because apparently he acknowledged the God of Israel as his God also (Num. 22 vs 18). But because of his greediness, he would rather go for the gift of man as his reward for his work as revealed in the book of 2 Peter 2 vs 15 and Jude 11. He may have gone astray searching for more powers outside the God almighty, and by that God left him unto his lust of his heart without depriving him of his gifts but waited until the day he would be condemned by the works of his hands. And eventually his greediness pushed him against God, and resulted in his death.

Through the testimonies of Israel from the time of their journey to their promise land, their case with Balaam son of Boer has been one of the outstanding

(Deut. 23 vs 4-6, Josh. 13 vs 22, 24 vs 9-10, Neh. 13 vs 2, Micah 6 vs 5).

He was a man that understood the language of the spirit, and also knew how to follow the heart of the Almighty God; *"He hath said, which heard the words of God, and knew the knowledge of the Most High ...."* He offered seven oxen and rams that he may reach God, that is, he knew how to reach God. The Bible says, *"When he saw that it pleases the Lord to bless Israel he went not, as at other times, to seek for enchantments, but set his eyes in the wilderness..."* toward the Israelites and for what he saw concerning them, he knew he will have to succumb totally for the Spirit of God Himself, as if it was that he has been prophesying initially with unwilling mind before that Numbers 24. However, he is cunning, greedy, and a rebel who will acquire riches in the destruction of others. I believe God knew him much in what he could do and that he is a dangerous man, God had to visited him to warn him of what he's about to do to His people.

This kind of people lives around us:

1. They are Spiritual robbers that trigger the physical robbery.

2. They are hired to monitor our lives. We may not notice them or know them at all, but they know us so well. For example, it's like a woman who was unable to conceive for so many years, but when the Lord would revealed the secret, He said the foundation of her problem can be traced to her mother, she had to protest that her mother was dead since when she was a little girl even before

she could think of anything called marriage. But God revealed that there had been a network of evil forces to monitor the curse of childlessness of which her mother has laid upon her through her life; from her home town to her office, and then to the environment she leaves. Those are the companies of Balaam.

3. They give counsel to obstruct our journey through there backbites and gossips

4. They are those ones who will pray, and patiently waits for your downfall to overtake you.

5. They are enviers of destiny.

And if we fail to detect such people or pray against them they may have gone before us to divert our journey or even capsize the vehicle of our destiny. And so I pray that every company of Balaam over your life shall be disappointed in Jesus name.

What the Israelites cannot understand about themselves and about God was being understood by this man called Balaam who has seen all what the Israelites need to see about God and concerning them. The words of Balaam to Israel show that there is a great plan of God for the Israelites.

Balaam's Words Concerning Israel in Numbers 23 and 24

This Balaam's words are obviously in four parts. And when they say the curses were turned into blessings, what I see is that some of this blessings are not a just-pronounced blessings but a blessings God had in place for them already in the beginning, since the days of their forefathers, it has being a reserved one from the time of Abraham; the blessings God has promised Abraham for his descendant. And now, for a man God Himself from His mighty throne has blessed already, how can he be cursed by any man. That was what Balaam tried to make Balak understand.

Now verses 9 and 10 of chapter 23 says: *"For from the top of the rocks I see him and from the hills I behold him: lo, the people shall dwell alone, and shall not be reckoned among the nations. Who can count the dust of Jacob, and the number of the fourth part of Israel? Let me die the death of the righteous, and let my end be like this."*

There goes the word of the man whose eyes are open; even though God deliberately put the word in his mouth, still, he didn't really see them as they were but he rather saw them as what they are really are in the spirit: what they will become; their strength, their potential blessings. This prophetical statement eventually came to pass. The literal fulfillment of this prophecy has been obvious during the more than thirty four centuries since it was spoken. The Jews has always being separated as a nation from other peoples. Though conquered many times, they have never been absorbed by their conquerors or lost their identity. Even also in this present world Israel has been surrounded by Islamic nations and yet they still remain predominantly as a Jewish nation (*....and shall not be reckoned among the nations...*).

Balaam inevitably proclaim them as a righteous nation seeing that the Almighty God is on their side; he wished his end could be like theirs. The Bible says if God is for us, who can be against us, who can judge us? The Bible says there is now no condemnation for those who are in Christ Jesus. Many times when God decides to be on one's favour it won't matter how weak and unworthy one may seems, God will still prove that person to be righteous, because God Himself is our righteousness. He says in His word in Isaiah 54 vs. 17 that *"No weapon that is formed against thee shall prosper; and every tongue that shall rise against thee in judgment thou shall condemn. This is the heritage of the servants of the LORD, and their righteousness is of me, saith the LORD".*

That is why we cannot condemn any anointed ministers of God—those who are really called, no matter how holier than them we may think we be, the Lord who has chosen them only has the right to judge them.

Moving further, as I said earlier that some of those blessings are already programmed one...In verse 19 of that same chapter 23 says, *"God is not a man that he should lie; neither the son of man that he should repent: hath he said, and shall he not do it? Or hath he spoken, and shall he not make it good?"*

There are so many promises for Israel, which God Himself cannot afford to let go. And since the promises are still intact no enchantment can reverse it. But this particular pronouncement in the passage above is the understanding Israelites themselves lacked because if they understood they wouldn't have turned from His ways. What God required from them is obedience as He has asked them in the book of Deuteronomy 28. We believers today, I exhort us to open our eyes that we might see through the promise of God who has called us, He never sleep neither slumber, He never slack in His ways, He will never reschedule His meeting time. All what He require from us is obedience and to diligently seek Him.

Balaam pronounced the Israelites' strength and their invasion as planned as revealed unto Balaam by God who is their strength. Verse 24 says, *"Behold, the people shall rise up as a great lion, and lift up himself as a young lion: he shall not lie down until he eat of the prey, and drink the blood of the slain."*

I am sure if the Israelites had heard this pronouncement, or better to say, if the Israelites could see what Balaam was seeing at that point in time it would have triggered them more to be courageous to face any adversary; they would have clung to God carefully and not be a stiff-necked, they would have put the whole of their trust on Him and obey Him wholeheartedly. It is not that God has not been giving them clues, in fact those signs and wonders God performed in their midst should be enough for them, but yet they could not perceive; they would not see.

As Balaam lifted up his eyes seeing the Israelites in their tent in chapter 24, he didn't just see an ordinary tent, he said, *"How goodly are thy tents, o Jacob, and thy tabernacles, o Israel!"*

And furthermore he prophesied about their strength and God's great backup in verses 8-9. *"God brought him forth out of Egypt; he hath as it were the strength of an unicorn; he shall eat up his enemies, and shall break their bones, and pierce hem through with his arrows He couched, he lay down as a lion, and as a great lion; who shall stir him up? Blessed is he that blessed thee, and cursed is he that curseth thee."*

And finally concerning what he saw about their achievement and their dominion of which the Israelites cannot see. They were once at the verge of it, but through their inability to perceive and their lack of knowledge with their God, they eventually prolong for themselves their destiny (more details in the next chapter). But let's see his last words upon Israel. *"I see him, but not now: I shall behold him, but not nigh: there shall come a Star out of Jacob, and a scepter shall rise out of Israel, and shall smite the corners of Moab, and destroy all the children of Seth and Edom shall be possession, Seir also shall be a possession of his enemies; and Israel shall DO VAILIANTLY and out Jacob shall come he that shall have dominion, and shall destroy him that remaineth of the city."*

The Israelites are meant to do valiantly; whether against any nation or in support with any nation, and already God has marked out their boundary for them even from the beginning when God has promised Abraham (Gen. 12 vs. 6, 7). They are meant to possess once the land God has prepared for them, their destination would have been for forty days and starts their lives afresh in prosperity, Moses would have entered there peacefully with his family, and for a long time he with Aaron would have been the judge and high priest......

In summary, the words of Balaam, son of Boer of Pethor onto Israel, are apparently into four parts which are:

1. *The greatness on the inside of Israel.*
2. *God's intervention over their lives.*
3. *Israel's potential strengths.*
4. *Israel's dominion.*

And now I will like every Christian to see in his or her condition what the Lord wants him or her to see, what God want you to perceive, what He is trying to let you understand. Do you still think God is incompetent, and that is why you have gone astray looking for alternatives? After so many signs and wonders you have witnessed, do you still trouble God to show you more signs for you to fully obey His instructions? Why can't you just pray that your eyes may be open that you may discover His mission for you; that you may know what you really are? Many Christian in their journey of life are still wondering around the wilderness just because they refused see. I tell you it is dangerous if you are still unable to see, if you are unable to perceive and understand. But I pray that your inner eyes shall be opened in the name of Jesus.

Chapter 3

WHAT YOU CHOOSE TO SEE

The book of Numbers chapters thirteen and fourteen tells us how some Israelites were sent to spy on the land the Lord Himself has promised them from Abraham, their father, of which God is ready to fulfill in their time. There is a great lesson we need to learn from this passage. *"And the LORD spake unto Moses, saying, Send thou men that they may search the land of Canaan, which I (already) give unto the children of Israel: of every tribe of their fathers shall ye send a man, everyone a ruler among them And Moses by the commandment of the LORD sent them from the wilderness of Paran: all those men were heads of the children of Israel."*

Verse 17 says, *"And Moses sent them to spy out the land of Canaan, and said unto them, Get you up this way southward, and go up into the mountain: and see the land, what it is; and the people that dwelleth therein, whether they are strong or weak, few or many; and what the land is that they dwell in, whether it is good or bad; and what cities they be that they dwell in, whether in tents, or in strong holds; And what the land is , whether it be fat or lean, whether there be wood therein, or not. And be ye of good courage, and bring of the fruit of the land. Now the time was the time of the first ripe grapes."*

In the passages read above, there are things I discovered about this errand God sent those people, God wanted this leaders to exercise faith by deciding themselves, what they will chose to see, that they might tell their people each tribe what they'll want them to believe, whether those people that dwells there are going to be strong for them or weak, many for them or few for them to conquered quickly, whether the land under any circumstances is going to be good or bad for them to dwell therein, or maybe the place where those people dwell can be pulled down like a tent or be a strong hold that can give them troubles to penetrate, and also to check if the land is so much affordable for them to dwell. But remember that God's statement *"...to search the land...which I give unto the children Israel..."* that is, God had already commissioned it for them. Why would God have to choose the tribe leaders for the spy work and not common men from the congregation? It's may be simply because this chosen leaders are those ones to encourage their tribe and to lead them to possess their possession for individual tribe respectively. That was why they were encouraged to be courageous.

Let's read further. Verse 21 says, *"So they went up, and searched the land from the wilderness of Zin unto Rehob, as men come to Hamath. And they descended by the south, and came unto Hebron; where Ahiman, Sheshan, and Talmai, the children of Anak, were. (Now Hebron was built seven years before Zoan in Egypt)*

The Man Whose Eyes Are Open

And they came unto the brook of Eshcol, and cut down from thence a branch with one cluster of grapes, and they bare it between two upon a staff; and they brought of the pomegranates and of the figs."

Verse 25 says, *"And they return from searching of the land after forty days."*

And after their journey they arrived with news and evidence, but what was their report?"

Verse 27 says, *"And they told him (Moses) and said, we came unto land whither thou sentest us, and surely it floweth with milk and honey, and this is the fruit of it Nevertheless the people are strong that dwell in the land and the cities are walled, and very great: and moreover we saw the children of Anak there The Amalekites dwell in the land of the south: and the Hittites, and the Jebusites, and the Amorites, dwell in the mountains: and the Canaanites dwell by the sea, and by the coast of Jordan."*

The Bible tells us that they went straight to Moses and Aaron at first to give the exact report of what they saw about the land and its people and they expressed their fear unto Moses and Aaron, forgetting that it was the Lord that sent them, and that the land was the one God has promised them and given them already. But the leaders were consumed with fear, and their fear evolved to be a rebellion, and with that they lead the heart of the rest of the congregation in rebelling instead of them to be an icon of faith and to encourage the rest of the congregation. They even decided to publicize their fear, and that the congregation may tend to them totally according to their rebellious heart; they had to exaggerate the news for them, as thus: Verse 32 *"....the land, through which we have gone to search it, is a land that eateth up the inhabitants thereof* (not flowing with milk and honey again); *and all the people that we saw in it are men of great stature And there we saw the giants: and we were in our own sight as grasshoppers, and so we were in their sight* (that is, they are able to crush them not even with their sword neither bows nor arrows but with their big foot)."

The rest of the congregation of Israel believed this negative report of the chosen leaders and they all rebel against God, why was it easy for them to do so? This is because sometimes we see things according to the context and condition of our heart; when we are consumed with fear we will definitely see negativity. Already, the Israelites had being tempting God initially and showing their lack of faith irrespective of great signs and wonders. The Lord said to Moses in Num 14:22: *"Because all those men which have seen my glory, and my miracles, which I did in Egypt and in the wilderness, and have tempted me now these ten times, and have not hearken to my voice."*

And by the time they could realize their foolishness they have lost the moment of their accomplishment.

But the Bible makes us to understand in this Numbers chapter 13:30 that Caleb among them all refused to see the way the rest of them are seeing things. He chose to understand God, and to see the way The LORD God Almighty has wanted them to see. Caleb said, *"Let us go up at once, and possess it; for we are well able to overcome it"* just because that's the way he have seen it. But as the whole congregation rose up to murmur against God and against Moses, Caleb (and eventually joined with Joshua) showed there sadness at the other's reaction but yet exhorted them...

Chapter 14:6-9 says, *"And Joshua the son of Nun, and Caleb the son of Jephunneh, which were of them that searched the land, rent their clothes: And they unto all the company of the children of Israel saying, The land, which we passed through to search it, is an exceeding good land If the LORD delights in us, then He will bring us into this land, and give it to us, floweth with milk and honey* (that is, if it's true that YAHWEH God who was the one that brought them out from slavery with His mighty Hand is still on their side, then He is the one who will do the finishing work) *Only rebel not ye against the LORD, neither fear ye the people of the land; for they are bread for us: their defense is departed from them, and the LORD is with us: fear them not"* (that is, with God on their side they could see how those in the land have become bread and how defenseless they are).

This were great words which qualified Caleb and Joshua to be worthy before the Lord God almighty that they might be those ones to enter the promise land amongst the chosen leaders and the rest who have murmured. But God who has being silent since the returned of those leaders spoke with the intention of destroying instantly those leaders and those that murmured, after the congregation took their rebellion to the extreme by trying to stone those who have pleased God by greatly acknowledging His majesty in their faith

(Heb. 11:12 *"But without faith it is impossible to please Him"*).

Verse 10 says, *"But all the congregation bade stone them with stones. And the glory of the LORD speared in the tabernacle of the congregation before all the children of Israel And the LORD said unto Moses.....I will smite them with the pestilence, and disinherit them, and I will make of thee a greater nation and mightier than they...."*

And with all the supplications of Moses, God still chose to destroy those that murmured starting with those leaders and then the rest.

What have we learnt so far from this passage? Have we found ourselves in this similar condition? There are two ways you will have to observe things: what you actually see and what you really chose to see whether is of negative and impossibility, or positive and possibility. This is the case of fact and truth: fact will tell you the way things are actually are, while the truth is the correctness of fact according to your own faith. Five or six Doctors may tell you evidently that it is impossible for you to walk again, or they may have told you that it is impossible for you to conceive due to some certain circumstances, but the truth according to your faith will tell you that with God all things are possible. Fact is situated with us humans while the truth is situated with God. But unfortunately, we humans only accept the facts' report that is why you'll see people die untimely death as a result of sickness. I feel sad when the Doctors will tell some people to put their houses in order; they will say, "Have fun, visit places, make charities, because sooner in less than three month you will die" even at their mid-forties or late fifties and they will accept easily only because they cannot see God in His faithfulness as He has promised in Psalm 91:16 that *"With long life will He satisfy us and shew us His salvation"*. Like the woman in the book of 1 Kings 3:21 when she was made to believe that her son was dead, she said, "But when I considered it in the morning, behold, which I did bear". That is she was able to identify her condition well by opening her eyes to see. New infant babies sometimes at first they may not give a definite form of face that will make us conclude that this how he or she looks like, or we may not even care to consider how they look, and that is why there are some cases of successful baby switching at birth. But the case of this woman is very different; she did not accept that report but she scrutinized it well and concluded that that dead child is not her baby. Likewise your case may be similar to other people who are hopeless but tell them your case is different because you don't have their eyes. Do not give in to those final evil reports, consider it so well, compare it with the promise of God and reject it and say, "When I considered it so well, behold, it is not mine".

Brethren, do not try to see your battle but try to see your potential victory, do not try to get weary by how far the journey is but rather be mindful of the joy at the finish line. There are enough eye opening promises of God in His Scripture. That is why the Bible says that we are not given the spirit of fear but of adoption whereby we can cry "Abba Father", because when fear sets in it will produce a negative prospect and an odd perception, and you not seeing rightly with God can lead to unfaithfulness and rebellion.

Also in relating to what we are saying in this chapter, God may ask us to do something we may think it is impossible, what God needs from us is an uncompromised obedience and not to be moved by sight. The case of Peter is another typical example in the book of Matthew 14:24-32. When Jesus walked on water, Peter asked Jesus to make him also walk on water of which Jesus permitted, but the Bible says, *"But when he saw the wind boisterous, he was afraid; and beginning to sink, he cried, saying, Lord, save me."* The question there is didn't he see the so-called boisterous wind before he asked Jesus to let him come? But at the middle of the faith exercise, he chose to see boisterous wind instead of fixing firmly his eyes upon the one who has asked him to come which wrought fear in him making him to doubt, and thus shrink his faith.

Hebrews 3 vs 8-12 says, *"(....Harden not your heart, as in the provocation, in the day of temptation in the wilderness: when your fathers tempted me, proved me, and saw my works forty years wherefore I was grieved with that generation, and said, they do always err in their heart; and they have not known my ways. So I swore in my wrath, they shall not enter into my rest). Take heed brethren lest there be in any of you an evil heart of unbelief, in departing from the living God."*

Departing from the living God is as saying not having the mind of God; not observing His intent, not acknowledging what He is capable of, despite the past great works of His hands, of which causes unbelief. So brethren, as you journey, always have faith in the Most High God for possibilities.

Many testimonies have revealed God to us more. His works in the scripture are authentic, and many of this works are meant for us that we may have faith in Him that He is the omnipotent God who is all sufficient. Even in the time of discomfort and challenge He said in His word that *"ye have not received the spirit of bondage again to fear: but ye have received the Spirit of adoption [the Spirit producing sonship] in [the bliss of] which we cry, Abba Father".* The rest of the 'blinded' elders of Israel didn't regard God as their salvation and strength, but only a momentary force that forced them out of Egypt. Likewise also, many so-called Christians today are like those Israelites that see God as an occasional cosmos force power? Or considering God to be a luck agent that is not consistent, that is why many eventually find themselves easily backslidden, succumbing to the ideology of Satan. Many rely on the works of their hands; they'll say I can't wait for God, where the word of the Lord has giving great hopeful orientation on those who will wait upon Him in Isaiah 40:31.

Trust in God; in His decision for your life, in His discretion towards you, and hold firm to His promise, and once again I say trust in God.

Chapter 4

THE REVELATION OF GOD IN THE SPIRITUAL BATTLE

In this passage, we shall be examining how God fight battles when we pray, how great His interference is in our battles. Do we really see how we escape any form of death? Do we ever perceive anything when we miraculously escaped any accident; whenever we stumble, or even fall on a little cause? Or whenever we notice unusual or strange feeling when passing through an area, do we really try to figure out what is really happening? I mean DO WE REALLY SEE ANYTHING? The truth is that there are many and great things God does for His people in the spirit even starting from the day you have decided to give your life to Christ and to follow Him forever. In the book 'Pilgrim Progress' by John Bunyan, there is a place there where the man called Christian wants to enter through a gate which at the top is written 'Salvation', and as he approaches the door slowly and knock, the guardian of it, as he saw Christian at the door ready to enter, quickly he pull him in, why? He says because there are arrows always fired at the entrance against the one who will enter, same as Christiana his wife. In there I knew that that is what really is going on in the spirit realm against anyone who will want to give his or her life to Christ. That is why you'll see people look convicted at first at the Gospel, and within seconds if not decided fast, they'll just say, "I'll think about it" or something may just occur that will disrupt the moment, and death may be the immediate consequence—the result of the arrows.

Like I always say, the moment we give our lives to Christ starts the battle of our lives against the world and against her master—Satan. This usually occurs not to the half-baked but those with the correct life: Job as been a very typical example, then the life of David, Moses and the Israelites against Pharaoh and Egypt (of which we shall discuss a little in this chapter) even Jesus the savior of the whole world against the scribes and against Satan himself, and so on.

What am I really saying? those little coughs, slight headaches, unexplained dizziness, strange and remarkable cobwebs attack, evil thoughts, evil urges and so on which may look casual may not be ordinary; it is not all of them that are normal, but also may be that a battle may be going on for you. There is a picture that really inspired me concerning this truth, in the picture is a man walking and towards him is a bird flying, but their shadows show something different; of the man is a shadow of a man (maybe an angel) holding a sword against the shadow of the bird which is actually a dragon. Rebecca Brown, M.D, in one of her books, says when we just wrestle in our prayers one may feel the effect in the physical body, which I believe is true.

Some personality in the Bible testifies to what I am talking about and gave a wonderful and an actual record about it without any exaggeration, they wrote it just the way they have seen it. This is where we should realize that all our praises are substandard before the Almighty God compared with His mighty works in our lives.

David

When we read 2 Samuel 22 and or Psalm 18, this chapter of Psalms was written by David when God delivered him from all his enemies and also Saul most especially. But does it really looks as if this Psalm was ascribed to his victory over Saul or anybody in particular, because I can't see the name Saul or any physical enemies being mentioned at all in the chapter? But it's as if what he really saw he defeated was something not really a flesh and blood but something so high in the spiritual order, I mean some principalities and powers, rulers of darkness in the high places. And the kind of victory he saw was very much powerful one, for how the LORD the Almighty God fought for him was a spiritual one of which one of the results was how he was delivered finally from Saul and some other of his enemies which includes Ahithophel, his son Absalom and his followers, Ishbosheth, even Abner and Joab.

David's eyes were opened so he could see and know that behind the physical battles was a great deal of demonic spiritual influences. However, in Psalm 18 from verse 1 to 3 tells of how he had seen God in his situation; how He had intervened in those spiritual engagements, he saw God fashioned Himself to play well the roles of these particular objects:

- A Rock that would break or cause a powerful effect on anything it hits. It revealed God as a powerful attacker, it also represents strength; it is reliable, immovable, and unshakeable. Any of it sizes can create a powerful and deep and lethal impact. They can be said to be a stone (because they are actually a mass of stone), or like the smooth stones David picked to fight Goliath. As we can see that if God wasn't really backing those stones up it would not have killed Goliath, no man could be so perfect that he will use a stone without any several tries but only at one chance to strike a man who is not still, deep at the center where there is a little space at the fore head. It can also show God to be our sustainer.

- A Fortress; a stronghold sufficient to create refuge for a larger number of people. As a king he would have known the importance and effectiveness of a fortress, maybe when in the battle the city with fortress would have often been the city that is difficult to attack; it's a place no enemy could just burst into in pursuit. And then again in 1 Samuel 22, the Bible tells us how David brought his families and those that are with him in the hold for refuge before he was told to leave there to go to the one God Himself had prepared for him in the forest of Hareth, and there afterward when he was in Keilah in 1 Samuel 23 God also told Him to leave there, and by that the Bible says, *"David and his men, which were about six hundred, arose and departed out of Keilah, and went whithersoever they could go....".* And in verse 14 the Bible made us to understand that he dwells in one of the wilderness' stronghold (the one God had prepared for him, again) where God hid him against Saul, and while in the cave of Adullam he reference the cave as the shadow of God's wing in Psalm 57:1. And at the stronghold in En-gedi also the Lord showed that He had delivered Saul into his hand, and so on. I believe these are what David remembered before concluding that God Himself is indeed his own fortress.

- A Buckler (Shield) for a powerful defense against any purposed and deliberate attacks, it stands between the attack and the victim that it may cause no harm. It may be that David remembered how God delivered him from one of the Philistines' warriors in 2 Samuel 21:15-17; when he almost fainted in the battle the giant even thought his great attack would have killed him, but God who was his shield had defended him.

- A High Tower where watchman stays that he might see the enemies' approach from afar off and give warnings against their attack. God often reveal every forthcoming attack to his people that they might know how to anticipate against it.

David experienced God in every of his battle, he would have perceived God Himself forming those things in the spirit realm and that may be why he has revealed God has the one who can play the role of what can serve has defense and security. It is like when a soldier calls God his gun or grenade or RPG, or a pilot soldier calling Him his jet fighter and that anything he aim will not miss and calling his jacket the Holy Spirit for defense and that any flying bullet will be missing him.

Have you ever seen God in your work; have you ever experienced Him beyond human comprehension in your secular job? When you just noticed that what you cannot do as a person or what you have never learnt about, you began to do it by an unusual inner force power. Some of this is what David saw and wrote concerning it.

An Adamant Host

Believe me as I say this, all what we could learn as a soldier of Christ can be seen in the life of David; to me he had being the pioneer and an icon of a prayer champion. These days people criticize how some Christians are violent in their prayers, they thought it to be cruel; they say, "After-all we were told that we should love our enemies". It's not that they are cruel, no, but it is our responsibility even from ancient times to [identify and] to get rid of anyone or anything that provokes our heavenly father to wrath through prayer. And furthermore, this is what I want us to learn from David himself, when he had the chances to kill Saul he didn't, as a matter love he had towards him. But do you know what? David understood that despite Saul's lethal threats he cannot afford to kill Saul using carnal weapon because he had regarded him as an anointed, but if we read David's Psalms concerning warfare especially in that Psalm 18, you will see that he had put his case before God, he said to Abishai to spare him, he said, *"As the Lord liveth, the Lord shall smite him; or his day shall come to die; or he shall descend into battle, and perish.* [But] *the Lord forbids that I should stretch forth mine hand against the Lord's anointed..."* That is to say, "Don't worry I have tabled his case before God that He might finish him."

But at the end he gave glory to God for his victory over Saul; he said in that Psalm 18:48 that *"He delivereth me from mine enemies: yea, thou liftest me up above those that rise up against me: thou hast delivered me FROM THE VIOLENT 'MAN'* (singular).*"* This has shown that even though David did not retaliate physically, he had been violent in his prayers not directly against Saul (because he had never mentioned his name in his Psalms) but every powers trying to bring him down, but since Saul had refused to repent he had to die along with it. That is why any man or woman who will not repent from his or her evil work, like Saul, will (one day) have to perish with his or her work; because this people have heard our Gospel, and we have revealed Christ the crucified unto them and prayed that there lost soul may be saved, yet they decide to dig a pit and break the hedge.

Since we, unlike 'the children of the bond woman' and other religious people, cannot afford to take physical actions against those afflicting us; depriving us our rights, even to serve our God then we will need to activate our spiritual weapon through our prayers, and I am sure for that reason, God did not take away the Old Testament from our Bible, because most of our weapons are installed there it is for us to go there and activate it in the moment of prayer.

David's Revelation

However, David knew his battles was more than what he has been seeing, everything was been engineered in the spirit realm, that is why he knew well that only God could perform the total deliverance from his enemies, so therefore he wrote in that Psalm 18:3 that *"I will call upon the Lord who is worthy of my praised: so shall I be saved from mine enemies"* He knew that no king can be saved by the multitude of his army, neither the mighty man can be delivered by his own strength for it is God Almighty that work out the victories. The Lord revealed what the people waging war against him were like; he understood that they are lions and those who are aflame; the sons of men whose teeth are spears and arrows, their tongues sharp sword. He knew that the powers from hell which tried to siege him in order to destroy his destiny were the brain behind those physical battles waged against him. He even admitted that those powers are too strong for him; the power that made him a renegade; a fugitive for many years and almost made him ally with the Philistines to go against his own country, and the power that revisited him again after he had become king and forced him out from his home. But David, unlike Job, he never thought his righteousness in God alone can save him but only a back up to his prayer warfare, but he said "as for me I will cry upon God, and He will save me".

The power from hell are terrible powers: they are the power of anti-Christ, they are great opposing powers that petition against us before God; they seek to terminate our destiny, these powers are stronger than us if not intervened by God Himself.

But in verses 6 through 15 of Psalm 18, he shared his testimony of his revelation about God in His vengeance: *"In my distress [when seemingly closed in] I called upon the Lord and cried to my God; He heard my voice out of His temple (heavenly dwelling place), and my cry came before Him, into His [very] ears. Then the earth quaked and rocked, the foundations also of the mountains trembled; they moved and were shaken because He was indignant and angry. There went up smoke from His nostril and lightning out of His mouth devoured; coals were kindled by it. He bowed the heavens also and came down; and thick darkness was under His feet. And He rode upon a cherub [a storm] and flew [swiftly] on with the wings of the wind. He made darkness His secret hiding place; as His pavilion (His canopy) round about Him were waters and thick clouds of the skies. Out of the brightness before Him there broke forth through His thick clouds hail stones and coals of fire.* Verses 13-15 says, *"The LORD also thundered in the heavens, and the Highest gave his voice; hail stones and coals of fire. Yea He sent out His arrows, and scattered them; and He shot out lightning, and discomfited them. The channels of waters were seen, and the foundations of the world were discovered at Thy rebuke, O LORD, at the blast of the breath of thy nostrils",* and then delivered him from his enemies like many waters.

It may be that all this great vision often appear to him in his dreams at the time of war or may come like a trance to him, or some sort of internal knowledge. I may not understand, but this I know that an ordinary man will not see this powerful revelation, but the man whose eyes are open.

Moses (and also the commentary of the battle between

Yahweh God and the several gods of Egypt)

Moses said in Exodus 15 that Jehovah is a Man of war; the God that fights the physical war from the spirit against their enemies especially Egypt. He said in Exodus 15:11, *"who is like unto thee O Lord, among the gods.... glorious in holiness and fearful in praises doing wonders"*. He acknowledged the kind of contest he had received from the gods of Egypt as a great one, even starting with the serpent contest.

In Egypt then, there were very powerful gods which they served, and there priest even then were regarded more powerful than Pharaoh because they are reckon with not only religiously but economically and politically, because they mostly control the heart and the mind of the people, they many times appear as there magicians and or wise men. The fact that God turned the rod into cobra suggests that He is the one who held true sovereignty (because cobra signifies royalty in Egypt) and swallowing that of those magician proves how He has subdued Ra's (the sun god of Egypt) supremacy because cobra was often refer to as 'The Fiery Eye Of Ra'.

All the ten plagues are purposely done by God to humiliate Egypt, her beauty, her power, and most especially her gods because that is one of their prides, truly we see ten plagues here but I see a contest. Pharaoh said to Moses, *"Who is the LORD that I should obey his voice to let Israel go? I know not the LORD, neither will I let Israel go"* and already the evil spirit of Egypt is backing it up, if it were not so the magician would not have counter Moses and Aaron before Pharaoh to prove that they also have back-up from some gods. God told Moses that only with mighty hand will Pharaoh released them because the evil power in operation surpassed the power of man, but how God will activate it was not discussed. But as Pharaoh has boasted against Yahweh the God of Israel signal a contest of power between his gods (about 25 or more, actually named below) and the one true God of Israel.

The battle commenced in Exodus 7:14-25 as He began with Khum, Hapi and Osiris which inhabited the Nile and rendered them powerless when Yahweh asked Moses and Aaron to smite the Nile River. And also humiliated Heqt (the frog spirit) in Ex. 8:1-15 by forcing people of Egypt who in their custom will not dare harm frogs in honor of Heqt, to now see frog as threat and began to kill it. And by duplicating these same acts of the plagues by their magicians they thought there gods are still intact. But when God will deal with Seb (or Geb the spirit dwelling in the Egypt's earth or dust) in Ex. 8:16-19, He ask Aaron to smite his (Seb's) head that it might bring lice, then their priest began to admit that Power supersedes power; they confessed *THIS IS THE FINGER OF GOD.*

Now, God saw that the battle was affecting His own people also He relieved Aaron's role in the battle and Moses to continue with it, and also put a great shield between His people and Egypt because He knew the next contest (with Uatchit, the Fly god of Egypt) in Ex. 8:20-32 would be more severe, which was the unleash of a great swarms of (blood sucking) flies, if Uatchit could prove himself, should stop the plague but of which he failed. Ptah, Mnevis, Hathor, Amon, Bast and also Khum were evil spirits that associates themselves with livestock like cows, bulls and with cattle and so on in Egypt, but they were defeated as they watch the livestock dies (Ex. 9:1-7).

Sekhmet, Serapis, and Imhotep were put into silence in Ex. 9:8-12 that even there priest this time, will not even appear in court before Moses because the Hand that worked with Moses was really heavy upon them; boils began to grow on the Egyptians.

Both Nut, the Egyptian's sky goddess, and Shu, the Egyptian god of the atmosphere, could not stop the hail of fire from heaven in Ex. 9:13-35.

Isis, Seth, Nepri, Ermute and Thermuthis are all associated with crops and harvest but could not protect them from the locust because they are powerless before the Almighty.

Ra or Amun-ra was the chief deity of all gods of Egypt and this demon was referred to as the sun god, God purposely dealt with him last; God, in turning the day into night made the Egyptians to see that with Him [Yahweh] the God of Israel all power must bow. At the process of the three days the people of Egypt would have been praying to Ra to give light, but the Bible says the darkness was so thick that they were not able to see each other, but on the other side of Goshen it was beautiful and sunning days, in other to tell the whole world in general that everyone who is on the Lord side will never be in darkness and vice versa, because He is the master of the universe.

Every Pharaoh in Egypt were all considered to be a deity also including the heir to the throne — first born for that matter, and that was why God told Moses again in chapter 10 that once again He will do one more plague that they will never forget in their entire life — God killed their first born son; with this plague God disgrace all their gods and tarnish the reputation of Pharaoh in the land.

And God crowned it all His dealings with Egypt by burying them in the Red sea. Moses had seen things the ordinary eyes could not see — he saw God in action and recorded some of it in Exodus 15. Note this statement in verse 1. *"....I will sing unto the LORD, for he hath triumph gloriously..."*

This has showed that there was a battle God had just finished; in verse 3 Moses said: *"The LORD is a 'Man of War': 'Yahweh' is His name."*

What made Moses call God a "Man of War"? Will he record what he had not seen or perceived God did? He didn't say, "God is a Miracle Worker", because He parted the sea [which of course anyone who didn't see more than that will give such record] but instead he called Him a 'Man of War' because he had seen more than that: he saw a blast from God's nostrils which made the sea to pile up and also saw the right hand of the Lord working wonders. Let's check out more of his testimony which he wrote in verses 6-7: *"Thy right hand, O LORD is become glorious in power: thy right hand, O LORD, hath dashed in pieces* [the power, the strength and pride of] *the enemy.*

And in the greatness of thine Excellency thou hast overthrown them (Egypt and her gods) *that rose up against thee: thou sentest forth thy wrath, which consumed them as stubble."*

Remember every one of Pharaoh's evil action was backed up by his gods who he would think by that he should prevailed, and never knew that he was to be the object of God's demonstration of power and to humiliate his gods.

But I love this part where Moses proclaimed in verse 11, that: *"Who is like unto thee, O LORD, among the gods? Who is like thee, glorious in holiness and fearful in praises, doing wonders? Thou stretchedst forth thy right hand, the earth swallowed them."*

To me, this actually has been a great record about God's potency that one cannot imagine unless one is in the spirit. Moses knew about life as a prince in Egypt, he knew the gods of Egypt are not mere idols but actually powerful evil spirits; he must have seen magicians performed in one of their ceremonies, and those spirits in act when summoned by their priests.

That may be one of the reasons why he was afraid initially to go back to Egypt, and that may be why God needed to introduced Himself in a spectacular way unto him that he may know that there is an all-superior God. But when Moses saw God's act in battle, he concluded that even this God of his fore-fathers is a Mighty Man of valor, and also reckoned that there is no other god like Him. Even through their journey in the desert when God gave them an angel to lead the way into the promise land, the Bible says the mountains skipped like rams and the little hills like lamb, that is, every challenges like mountain such as Balak and Balaam, wall of Jericho, Amalekites and so on; those they had great battles with even the giants of Canaan and her neighboring cities which Joshua defeated. And when I was thinking about their journey in the wilderness I thought truly if there is no divine intervention they would not have survived; because therein is the abode of some wild and poisonous animals, gangs of outlaws which could robbed them of their gold and silver and their livestock, savages and so on which can be a problem [like little hills] to them but there is no record of such attacks; their children were not kidnapped no one got lost, and no sort of any animal's attacks (except the serpent God Himself sent to them when they sinned) because they had all 'skipped like rams'.

Little wonder why David and Moses have had some most wonderful odes of praises in honor to this Great God in their Psalms. We need to see God in action when He answers our prayer, when we see God in His act we are going to upgrade confidence in God and increase our praises and worships in reference to Him.

The angels in heaven according to the book of Revelation, are not tired of praising this wonderful God; they always sing holy, holy, holy to the God Almighty because He appears wonderful and awesome at every seconds glance at Him.

Baal and Yahweh at Mount Carmel

Baal has been a rival of Jehovah God in Israel since the time they have entered Canaan. When Gideon was named Jerubbaal (let Baal contend, plead, fights against him) he didn't reject the name until Baal — this evil spirit took vengeance on him after Gideon himself return to idolatry, this gave Baal the upper hand to operate properly but in the life of his children, the Israelites after he died did not honor him neither give any regard to his family; his seventy children was murdered by a bastard amongst his children, etc.

Baal was a powerful idol of the Canaan land. But in 1 Kings, God raised Elijah for a great contest against Baal on Mount Carmel, and on that day Baal was silenced. Those idols are usually demonic, they can be summoned for a particular request and it will respond, but not when God is present at that situation. Elijah in his confrontation said to Ahab and the prophets of Baal *"And call ye on the name of your gods, and I will call on the name of the LORD: and the God that answereth by fire, let him be God."* I believe if Baal had never answered them before then they won't have bothered themselves in accepting Elijah's challenge not mentioning cutting themselves for Baal to respond, but Baal was silenced before Yahweh, Almighty God the creator of heaven and earth when He answered by fire. Every idol are not actually impotent, when an idol is been sculptured as an object of worship, every of it conjure especially with a blood sacrifice will be utilized by demons because God will never answered through them. That was why God warned the Israelites that when He was talking to them at Mount Sinai he didn't appear to them in any similitude and by that they should never represent Him with any image; because they promotes familiar spirit, witchery and wizardry, magical powers, necromancy, palm reading, and all these are what God commanded Israel not to practice.

But, However, whenever God gets involved with them they have no choice but to keep quiet and become impotent; having eyes but cannot see, and having ears but never hear, because the demon behind them cannot stand His presence so they will have to leave the objects.

The Steady Invisible Host

2 Kings 6:15 says, *"And when the servant of the man (Elisha) of God was risen early, and gone forth, behold a host compassed the city both with horses and chariots. And his servant said unto him, Alas, my master! How shall we do? And he (Elisha) answered, fear not: for they that be with us are more than they that be with them."*

Many lives of Christians has been like the case of Elisha's servant who cannot see. This often happens as a result of fear, even after the promises of God for protection in His word, yet they will still be intimidated by the witches and wizards. Assuming if Elisha did not pray for his eyes to be opened, what could have happened to this young man? But the Bible says he saw: and, behold, the mountain was full of horses and chariots of fire round about Elisha — steadily; they are ready to strike any man at the command of Elisha. So also if God would open our spiritual eyes, then we will know that there is a greater heavenly security greater than that of the world's president; the bodyguard up there does not let anything even the tiniest object escape there sight, there counter terrorist unit does not fail to identify, and their responds are in seconds, they are not bias but follow strict order and respond only to the Master God and His children, they don't relent neither retreat, there handcuff can never be breached and their security can never be compromised, they are not corrupt but always on alert, and to crown it — they have never lost any battle. That is why we are well convinced that Christ willingly gave Himself to be crucified because He would have called upon those heavenly hosts. Only one was given to the Israelites to lead on through the wilderness and prepare the way in Exodus 23:20-23, and thus having a smooth passage at the result.

Activating the Power as of Old

The Bible says in the book of Revelation woe unto the inhabitant of the earth because Satan [the accuser of the brethren is being thrown down there. There are unexplainable cases that we cannot afford to turn the side of negligence to: strange footage in our world presently, that only a fool will see it as hoax or superstition, manifestations such as; UFOs, the called Big foot, leprechaun, mermaids and mermen and some gruesome creatures of fairy tales: ogres, trolls, jinn, etc. Yes, I believe they are not superstition but they are actually the fallen ones or spelled victims. They can also be noticed when any domestic animal behave in an unusual or extreme cruel ways.

But Satan possessed man has the most terrible havoc and casualties, using religion, self-centeredness, love of money, lust for power, and so on, this has caused war: civil war, national crises — anything you could name it, and many helpless people are being involved in the killing and millions of lives always be at stake. Even in the government, there are conspiracies victimizing her people in order to fulfill her selfish ambition. Another great target is the family; he knew two wrong persons in a wrong relationship, creating a wrong family will eventuate into a wrong nation. All this are not natural, but they are backed up with evil spirit. Some (it may not be all but most of it) so called natural hazard or global warming so to say are backed up with supernatural powers, those outbreak diseases; unexplainable plague in the ages past and those incurable diseases of this present time. If it is not a punishment from God then it must be demonical, because the devil is always there to destroy the works of God.

But this I know that the power of God in the ancient times is still intact it is for us to activate it in the sweet moment of prayers, we need to activate the power of God as it is written for us to acknowledge: the right hand of God that dashes the enemies in pieces; the voice of God that breaketh cedars of Lebanon; the fire that consumes the unrepented nations; the strike of the Holy Ghost; the smite of the angel of the Lord; and the mercy that rejoices over judgement to avail mightily for us over the evil governments, tyranny and terrorism, corruption and conspiracy, the lust for power and selfish interest; over ancestral curse and broken families; over outbreak diseases, spread of viruses even by animals and over starvation, and so on respectively as they deserved. And as God has fought for His people in ages past so also He can do today because He has never changed, only if we go to Him humbly with boldness and faith in our supplication.

Chapter 5

SEEING THE POTENTIAL

Do not forget in this book, we are trying to talk about things hidden to man but which we should see as children of God when our eyes are open of which potential is included.

What is potential? This is simply an unrealized ability; but in the spiritual sense of it, it is a thing that determines ones destiny, it is a treasure or a seed ought to be discovered fast. Some potential are easily noticed and quick to observed, while some are unable to be seen by simplicity and very hard to discover. There is a potential danger and a potential benefit, and it leads to diver of paths in the destiny of life. Some potential are talents, some are strengths, and some are weaknesses, some are a specific evil deed (the so called "the animal in man"), and some are a specific righteousness. Some are discovered by oneself, some are discovered by people (wise, parents, siblings, mentors, and even the enemies), and some are discovered by revelation (from God). Potential can be triggered by the influence of environment, position, conditions (maturity, etc.), and pressure of any kind.

Some of this is what I will be analyzing in this chapter. In this chapter I will like us to really seek the face of God in prayers to open our eyes unto potentials in our lives that it may be easy for us to fulfill our purpose and to be able to deal with our lives correctly that it may yield us good fruit, because we really need God to open up our eyes unto these things in our environments and also most especially in our lives. What do I mean by seeing our potentials or what do I want us to understand? This is as saying seeing our self, because sometimes we may be thinking that we cannot end up behaving in some particular way either positively or negatively of which eventually we may be disappointed with ourselves and this may take an effect in our destiny. There are some similar cases in the Bible that I will want us to examine, about how those potential are discovered.

Potential Discovery By Revelation

Let us look into the case of Elisha and Hazael in the book of 2 Kings 8 vs. 7-15. Hazael has never seen himself as a killer. He appeared at first as a young innocent man with no bad motive within him, he has been a faithful servant to his master, King Benhadad of Syria, and how do I know? Because being the only one the king could send at that very particular point in time, then Hazael must have earned the king's trust by his service. But he never knew himself; but the day his master sent him to Elisha was the day God exposed what he would really be, and that day without hesitation he unleashed the animal in him. He never knew he would deliberately bring death to his master. But let's read what the Bible says; *"And he (Elisha) settled his countenance steadfastly, until he was ashamed: and the man of God wept. And Hazael said, why weepeth my lord? And he answered, because I know the evil that thou wilt do unto the children of Israel: their strong holds wilt thou set on fire, and their young men wilt thou slay with sword, and wilt dash their children, and rip up their women with child."*

And at the hearing of this barbaric act predicted on him he declined even with humble heart, because he had never had this in heart in his lifetime, and apparently he had never think about it. He replied; *"And Hazael said, But what, is thy servant a dog, that he should do this great thing?"* (He even classified as dog anyone who will do that because he had never imagine such an act to be done by any reasonable man). *"And Elisha said the LORD hath showed me that thou shall be king over Syria."*

Brethren, like I said we really need to ask God to help us reveal our true selves unto us that we may know how to handle ourselves in anticipation to the future consequence; let youths pray about their future selves, let the older ones pray for their children.

This man, Hazael, doesn't know what awaits him which will warrant him to fulfilling those barbaric acts. But as soon as he learnt he was going to be king, immediately everything about him began to change. The Bible reveals that without another word he left. And on the next day he already knew what to do; he knew (the strategy) how he would do it, where to do it and when to do it, without anyone's supportive idea or effort as if wasn't his first time.

"And it came to pass on the morrow, that he took a thick cloth, and dipped it in water, and spread it on his face, so that he died: and Hazael reign in his stead."

Elisha predicted what he would do to the Israelites, but the question is did he also predicted what he was going to do to his master king Benhadad as well? What he did to his master as revealed his tendency and capability of what he has never imagine himself doing. And all this prediction he later did in 2 Kings 10 vs. 32-33, the Bible says he oppressed Israel in 2 Kings 13 vs. 22. This discovery is a revelation from God. We can as well tell God to show us our real self; what we could be capable of, because Satan always works against someone's spiritual sight until they have reached their destruction they won't be able to see anything.

Potential Discovery By Oneself

In the book of 1 Samuel 17, David trusted in his instinct coupled with his faith in God when he realized his potential he was able to face Goliath and defeated him. To his brother, David was a weakling because they didn't really know him and they couldn't really see what he was capable of. But David knew himself and was courageous in God.

Read Verse 23. *"And as he* (David) *talked with them, behold, there came up the champion, the philistine of Gath, goliath by name, out of the armies of the philistines, and spake according to the same words* (he has been speaking since the past forty days): *and (on the day he will be put to shame) David head them" And all the men of Israel, when they saw the man, he fled from him, and were sore afraid."*

Verse 26 says, *"And David spake to the men that stood by him, saying, What shall be done to the man that killeth this philistine, that he should defy the armies of the living God?"*

In this passage there was a particular pressure on Israel and those that think they are strong showed who they really are — a coward. Sometimes some people will display their muscle as one who has strength, but deep within them there is a cowardice spirit. Some people jump here and there on the altar making mouth but on the day of test they weep like a baby.

The day Goliath showed up revealed the kind of people on the battle field: the fearful, weak and faithless in God. But as that revealed the weakness in rest of the Israelites, it revealed the strength (the potential) on the inside of David, for forty long days did Goliath terrified the whole of Israel, no warrior could challenge him, no prophet could stimulate the people, and no king could encouraged, Saul even sounded dissuading when he asked David to put on armor against Goliath. But Goliath's terror ended on the day the man who knew God, whose eyes are open, who trust his instinct coupled with faith upon the LORD only, was sent to the battle field but only to go on a food errand to his brothers on the battle field.

He said in verses 32-38, *"And David said to Saul, Let no man's heart fail because of him; thy servant will go and fight with this Philistine.* (And that is instinct). *And Saul answered and said to David, thou art not able to go against this philistine to firth with him: for thou art but a youth, and he a man of war* (discouragement 1) *and David said unto Saul, Thy servant kept his father's sheep, and there came a lion, and a bear, and took a lamb out of the flock: And I went out after him, and delivered it out of his mouth: and when he arose against me, I caught him by his beard, and smote him, and slew him Thy servant slew both the lion and the bear: and this uncircumcised philistine shall be as one of them* (he knew he potential he carries), *seeing he hath defied the armies of the living God. David said moreover, The LORD that delivered me out of the paw of lion, and out of the paw of a bear, he will deliver me out of the hand this philistine* (that's a faith in God for the finishing). *And Saul said unto David, Go, and the Lord be with you." And Saul armed David with his armour, and he put an helmet of brass upon his head; also he armed him with a coat of mail* (which is the discouragement 2)".

The anointing of God through Samuel over David's life wrought a powerful potential into his life, he knew it and by faith he worked towards it. Of course David didn't rely only on his instinct and experience but looked unto God for the finishing work he was not a coward like others just because he could see: what he possessed.

We Christians need to know what is inside of us that the enemies may not cheat us. Christian race is not a bread and butter race, it is a battle for survival and the violent take it by force, and by the virtue of that, the Lord has endowed every children of God with power to sustain us through the journey but it is for us to activate it with faith.

And now brethren, have you discover yourself in God, are you still been intimidated by the enemies, have you discover the power within you? Apply the Word of God, and then picture that mountain before you as your stepping stones to your greatness, and subject that goliath before you under your feet and move forward by fire.

Potential Discovery By Others

David called his son Solomon in 1 Chronicle 28:9, he said; *"And thou, Solomon my son, know thou the God of thy father, and serve him with a perfect heart and with a willing mind: for the LORD searcheth all hearts, and understandeth all imagination all imaginations of the thoughts: if thou seek Him, He will be found of thee: but if thou forsake him, he will cast thee off forever."*

David as a father to Solomon knew his son so well. Even before he prayed to God for wisdom in 1 Kings 4, David knew his potential as a wise person when he asked him for the judgement on Joab and Shimei in 1 Kings 2. He said to him in verse 6 that "according to thy wisdom" and in verse 9 "for thou art a wise man" that is, Solomon already has a feature of a wise and David knowing it was able to commit the judgement of Joab, Shimei and others into his hand confidently, of which he executed wisely. David gave warnings to his son, Solomon, and revealed to him that whatsoever a man could boast of about his work for God, what matters most is his heart toward God, David knew his son to be resolute in his ambitions, if it were not so he wouldn't have told him to be careful about his thoughts and imaginations (that is, his intentions), that he might put God first. God also instructed him in corresponding to what David his father had told him when he was at the success in building the house of the LORD in 1 Kings 6:11-13. *"And the word of the LORD came to Solomon, saying, concerning this house which thou art in building, if thou wilt walk in my statutes, and execute my judgement and keep all my commandments to walk in them; then will I perform my word with thee, which I spake unto David thy father: and I will dwell among the children of Israel, and will not forsake my people Israel."*

Here, despite the building of the temple, yet God told him and said "what you are doing right now (even though it looks nice) is not really important to me, but to walk in my statutes and judgement". But at the end Solomon disappointed God.

He at first set a higher ambition upon himself than God; even though the primary purpose for him is to build the house of God, David didn't really say anything about building the palace but laid more emphasis on the building of the temple, but reverse was the case; he built the palace which is his own house for thirteen years, when he built the temple which is the house of GOD for only seven years, he built his own house 100 cubits length, 50 cubits breath and 30 cubits height, but the house of GOD 60 cubits length, 20 cubits breath and 30 cubits high, and so on.

People came from all over the world to see the wonders of his wisdom and not the God who gave him the wisdom, they came to see the beautiful Israel he had built, and not the God who is the author of the success of Israel, all attractions are on Solomon the wise and his kingdom the rich and great nation, with beautiful temple but second to the most beautiful palace. He however was not contented with the wisdom God gave him but went on further in searching for wisdom with the pagans; married them and served their gods. He said in Ecclesiastes 1:17, *"And I gave my heart to know wisdom, and to know madness and folly: I perceived that this also is a vexation of the spirit"* and he went on further and said *"For in much wisdom is much grief: and he that increaseth knowledge increaseth sorrow".*

This I know, that the wisdom of God can never bring grief or sorrow, or be vanity unless one contaminated it with the worldly affairs.

We parents really need to give time to detect the potential greatness and the potential weakness of our children not only on what they would love to become in the future as career according to the display of talents but also in their persona with the application of wisdom and prayer for revelation.

We should always give a microscopic look into every behavior, every little change in them and every little development of our children, spouses, co-workers, friends and so on that we may know how to anticipate well against the end product. The Bible says if anyone is in need of wisdom let him ask. By the wisdom of God we are able to detect and to handle every cases of potential by their act to do in advance to the effect; could it be that we need to pray concerning it, could it be that we need to tutor someone on what you have observe in him or her, or could it be that we are the one to make some changes from us toward them, all these is what the wisdom of God will help us to know. I always tell people when the boys in the family are behaving somehow to their sisters or vice versa or whenever there is a quarrel that if you guys could behave to your sisters or mother like that then how will you behave to your wife? I always urge the sisters to manage their brothers as they are going to manage their husband, in other words they should starts their marital training right with their people in their nuclear family; managing the habits of each other.

Seeing It Coming

When God open our eyes we will discover also that many things surrounding us can be a potential danger. When the bible says flee from the appearances of evil, it is talking about us recognizing what could become evil and run away from it. When a wall is cracked and crumbs begins to fall from it then you should know that it is giving a collapse sign. Sometime ago, we lived in a particular old building house, and we lived on the top story of the building, at that place we had no kitchen, so we performed everything supposed to be done in the kitchen at the backyard, down steers, most especially the washing of plates, we got tired of going up and down packing plates, so we decided to be washing the plates at the up steer's verandah we even washed clothes also, and every water falling out of those washes flowed down on the wall and by that the wall kept absorbing in the waters, we were warned so well about the act but we ignore those warnings, until one day the wall got soaked with all those water and the patches on the wall began to fall off. But thank God one of the tenants living below where it affected most was not a negligent type so he quickly pack some of his belongings and left the apartment, and not quite long after in the middle of the night the wall broke down and the one quarter of the house collapsed, at that very midnight some tenant got themselves packed out. My point is if that brother had not seen it coming and reacted to it, he would have died.

So also we have many warnings that those the Lord as set as a watchman for us may have been giving us, but many Christians today usually disregard warnings and mainly out of their "holy pride"; they'll say, "Who are you to give us warning" despite the fact that the little analyses that buttress the warning is genuine, yet discrimination causes them to look down on him, and reject him, they will not even want to hear a youth to say, "thus saith the Lord" they will reply like, "Who are you? Is your father not Mr. 'John bull'? Common, we know when your parents gave birth to you" and as a matter of fact, they did that to Jesus also.

Remember, some prophets of the Old Testament were ignored when they give warnings about the coming destruction, of which eventually came to pass. Jesus also in Matthew 24 gave prophesy about both tribulation in Jerusalem and world's end when He shall come at the second time, He said in verse 34 that that particular generation will not pass away until the prophesy come to pass. In 70 AD the prophesy in Jerusalem came to pass and those that knew and did not disregard Jesus warnings quickly took to their heels as Jesus did command them (giving reference to the prophesy in the book of Daniel) which he says: *"When ye therefore shall see the abomination of desolation, spoken of by Daniel the prophet, stand in the holy place, (whoso readeth, let him understand:). Then let them which be in Judaea flee into the mountains: Let him which is on the housetop not come down to take anything out of the house. Neither let him which is in the field return back to take his clothes."*

But everyone who took the warning slightly were killed. It was even told that a man who was rich in those time wrap up all his gold and money and hided it under his clothe and swallow some and thus made his stomach seemed bigger and was unable to run fast, and by the time he was struck with spare all those coins and gold gushed out with his intestine, and as those Roman soldier saw it they concluded that anyone with big stomach would do the same and that gave them green to attack most the people with big stomach and that included the pregnant women and that made to pass what Jesus said that "Woe unto them that are pregnant".

So brethren, when warning comes do not disregard it but look to it prayerfully, irrespective of the vessel.

- **Strange feelings and unusual behavior**

Sign often comes sometimes when evil would befall on someone (especially believers) from Satan, which is why it is very advisable for people not to disregard it whenever they often have strange feelings, or like a heavy burden, sending them an unusual signal. Like the man who said, "Before my wife had the accident that claims her life her behavior changed; she prayed more than ever before which is very unusual to me". And also a woman said before her husband died she noticed that he did what he had not being doing before: he went to fetch water with his children, had a big play time with them of which she was surprised about, but at the next day the man died. Not that this people had known that death is coming, but the inner being (which is their spirit) was the one trying to tell them something of which they eventually could not understand. As a Christian we should be very much in alert in the spirit; working on every strange feelings. There was a time I was going to play lawn tennis as usual every Saturday mornings, then, but on that day on my half way there I felt a strange feeling which I've never felt before whenever I'm going to the tennis court, but that day I started pleading the blood of Jesus, and at the end of the day I only got one of my tooth chipped at the result of a serious accident on the court that day; out of little or no cause I got blacked out, the last thing I could remember was trying to return a lobbed service much higher than me, later found myself face-down on the ground after gaining consciousness by the shout of people in the court and not knowing what has happened, but I saw blood on my shirt and my lips bruised by my chipped tooth. I thought to myself by this kind of accident I should got my neck broken or got two or three teeth removed, but thank God I was not injured as such, because I have perceived earlier through my feeling that something was coming and by the grace of God I got myself defended by the blood of Jesus.

Like I said, we Christians should always give a microscopic look on every unusual matter; we should always be at alert as the 1 Peter 5:8 tells us. When some husbands bring a strange woman and calling her secretary, or some ladies calling another man who is not her partner, best friend, then one should be highly sensitive in the spirit. There will be a situation where some women should pray and snatch there husband away from the hook of the devil instead of holding grudge against him, or they'll say that's the way marriage is–struggling. For we wrestle not against flesh and blood not your spouse that is not cooperative nor the child that is wayward. The time people need to face the devil that he might flee will be the time they will be running helter-skelter, and the time when people need to flee, that is the time they will be proving smart and strong, doing right thing at the wrong time, these are the results of spiritual blindness. There is a time we pray for help from God, and there is a time we exercise the power God has given us; there is a time to bind and there is a time to loose.

- **_Dreams as our monitor_**

Dream is very important in the life of man, it is a medium where God often speak with people to warn and to reveal things that are hidden to man be it things that are past or things yet to come. It is a means by which God talk to every man: Christian or not, therefore if God could reveal something through dreams to people who are unbeliever, and you as a Christian you are unable to hear from God and yet you are unable to dream dreams, then it is very dangerous because Satan has blinded you to become an ignorant that he might cheat you.

It was through dreams that God had revealed things to some people who eventually became great in the Bible. It was that means that Joseph knew his future, it was through dreams and its interpretation Daniel was regarded as the greatest and wisest in the strange land even among those people who saw themselves as wise. Even in the New Testament, it was a guide to the apostles like Paul and Peter for their missions.

In Joel 2:32, the Bible says the old people will have dreams so it is also the will of God for persons to have dreams, of which if you ask me I would say it is a blessing unto every man, and which also exhibit the love of God to every human.

And there's no doubt that as God uses it, Satan also could manipulate it. But every dream from God will not wrought insanity into one's mind nor go contrary to His word, but usually warning, and also it is a revelation about what someone should know; a vision concerning one's future of which many cases are in the Bible. If you read some Christian books or literature about dreams you will see how it has become help for people. If only thing you can do is to dream regularly as a Christian doesn't make you an inferior amongst others, it pleases God to talk to you only through it and make it your spiritual monitoring system. So from today hence forth do not disregard or consent to people who disregard dreams.

Chapter 6

SEEING FROM GOD'S ANGLE (Mystery in God's Will)

The Bible says in Jeremiah 29:11, *"For I know the thought that I think towards you, saith the LORD, thoughts of peace, and not of evil, to give you an expected end"*. Our God is not cruel in His decision toward His people, when He says He will do something the best thing is to count it unto Him for righteousness; "Thy will be done" and "to obtain mercy" should always be our best prayer as a believer in most of our unpleasant situation. There is no iota of unrighteousness in God, there are some cases in the Bible that one might just think it's unfair, but if we would understand God we will need to patiently meditate on the decision He makes, and thus we will eventually see that everything in God has a purpose, and in His purpose lies a special message for everyone that follows Him. When God says in His word, "Jacob have I loved and Esau have I hated", the Bible says in Romans 9:14, 16 concerning that *"...is there unrighteousness with God? God forbid, for He saith unto Moses, I will have mercy on whom I have mercy, and I will have compassion on whom I will have compassion, so then it is not of him that willeth, nor of him that runneth, but of the God that showeth mercy".*

Most of the time when God seems to be cruel in His ways to people, it is because they lack understanding, and refused to consider why, that is the reason why the infidels many times question the authority of the Bible and the truth about God's existence. But the fact is, whenever man refuses to give God His regards then God will revealed Himself by Himself: Pharaoh disregarded the God of Israel in the book of Genesis and God used Him to demonstrate His power; Herod in the book of Acts of the Apostles when displaying himself has a god, was struck by the angel of the living God, and so on. An adage says, "a war foretold will not implicate a (wise) cripple" that is, when we give regard to the warnings and observe carefully the instructions of God then we are safe.

When God does something or decides to do something which may seem unpleasant to us, before thinking as an infidel that God is unfair let us put this into consideration: that I'm I the one who is in error; have I taken a wrong step, or have I gone away from the presence of God? If not, then what do I need to understand in that certain situation. Sometimes God will want us to understand and to admit it that He is still God in every situation, and sometimes God will want to convey message in that certain situation for us to learn. But I tell you, you cannot really see perfection in God's decision unless you see from His angle and failure to do that it may be dangerous, how? I got a few examples from the Bible. God told Moses in Numbers 14:11-12, *"And the Lord said unto Moses, How long will this people provoke me? And how long will it be ere they believe me, for all the signs which I have shown among them? I will smite them with the pestilence, and disinherit them, and will make of thee a greater nation and mightier than they."*

If you are Moses would you have done the same thing Moses did — interceding for them? That may seems to be a good heart, but unto God's dissatisfaction, why did I say that? Because God never changed His mind on this decision against the rebellious Israelites after Moses' plead, but only postponed it, verse 23 of the same chapter revealed God saying, *"Surely they shall not see the land which I swore unto their fathers, neither shall any of them that provoked me see it…".* The Bible revealed that they all died one after the other in the wilderness. Truly the Lord is slow to anger but He also have a cup of wrath which man's iniquity drips in when there is no true repentance (Rom. 9:22; Rev. 15:1, 7; 1 Thess. 2:16) and when it is full there will be no remedy (2 Chr. 36:16). The LORD told Abraham in Genesis 15:16 that the time his seed shall possess their land, then, the iniquity of the Amorites would have been full, that is why I said God is always righteous in His decision. But if Moses could have seen from God's angle he would have known that those people would later be a snare unto him. Not quite long ago in Numbers 20, these same people of Israel provoked Moses into anger to the extent that according to Deuteronomy 32:51; he dishonored God's name by disregarding God's simple instruction which made him to lose the Canaan land destination eventually. He begged God concerning it.

He said in Deuteronomy 3 vs 26, *"But the LORD was wroth with me for your sakes, and would not hear me: and the LORD said unto me, let it suffice thee* (that is, enough of his plea!); *speak no more unto me of this matter."*

God shut out Moses' pleas basically because Moses had hindered God's righteous judgement thinking his opinion was more reasonable, but unable to see from God's angle; he should have perceived that the Israelites are obstinate and will not cease to tempt God. Moses whose record was *"...the man Moses was very meek, above all the men which were upon the face of the earth"* but was broken by the stiff-necked and stubborn headed Israelites he once pleaded for to the detriment of the completion of his task. I believe that it is still God's will for him and his own desire to enter into the promise land. There are many people you cannot waste your time interceding for, when it seems that the heaven is closed on your request on somebody then God want you to see some things, many such cases has been shared as an experience by some men of God I knew, that God will even tell them that if they tarry longer in praying for that particular sick person not to die they will die along-side with that person. Remember God, when Samuel was still mourning for Saul, He said to Samuel to stop mourning and that He had rejected him already (even after his second year on the throne), even though thereafter, Saul still spent several years (like thirteen years) on the throne.

Apostle Paul prayed to God to deliver him from a certain infirmity but the answer he received was *"my grace is sufficient for thee."* But Paul knew it was eventually a good makeup for him that he might fulfill God's purpose through it. But in the case of Hezekiah, who thought God was unfair when He said he would die, he averted it with his prayer out of his broken heart, he didn't even ask why God suddenly came up with such a decision because there was no record of a particular sin from him. But when God later gave him fifteen years longer life, at the process of it he did really mess up: in proudness of his heart he exposed Israel's riches and the temple treasure unto the heathen out of the will of God (2 Kings 20:12, 13; 2 Chron. 32:27, 31), he expressed how selfish he was when he considered his punishment will be in the time of his children in 2 Kings 20:19, and gave birth to the worst king ever in the history of Israel — King Manasseh, even though he later repented, but that was after he had been the first king to send himself and along with the children of Israel to their first exile, and according to 2 Kings 24:3, his sins was once again recounted to be the cause of the second great exile.

It's a pity many Christian's prayer (even out of their honest, kind and sober heart) has been a snare to their own lives, many have averted the decision of God to the detriment of their lives, as a matter of fact no one have a good and justifiable reason before God. If we believe it is the righteousness of God that justifies then why will you think you will have a genuine reason for questioning God's final decision. Remember, the Bible says the foolishness of God is wiser than the wisdom of man. Many Christians are fond of saying, God can never ask you to do this or that; like the popular mentality that God cannot ask you [a good Christian] to go into politics even though you can vote in the election, or saying why would God asked you to pray that some enemies waging war against you that they might die (only if they refused to repent), okay, if it seems absurd then why would Jesus said, in Matt. 18:6, to tie a millstone around the neck of (only) an offender of little ones and to be thrown inside the sea, is it to live or go there and repent? I think not, but definitely a death sentence, when Peter said to Saphira that they will soon carry her own corpse also, those that just carried her husband's, don't you think she can still repent before those people arrived? They say, "It was so that those in that time might fear the Holy Spirit". What about now-a-days? Should the Holy Spirit be disrespected? Then we can also tell our Christian brothers to resign themselves from civil defense and militia jobs to avoid killings. Of course, God is love and merciful but He is also a Great Avenger who is awesome and dangerous in His ways against the unrepentant nations. Sometimes God's job for someone often seems irrational and some fellow Christian brethren will question your sanity. When God called John the Baptist, people thought he had an evil spirit; Hosea was caused by God to marry a prostitute to fulfill his mission, and so on. But this I know, God will never ask you to do anything contrary to His Word, and anyone who had called himself or herself into ministry will never last, and anyone who uses his own wisdom to do God's work will never succeed. But every pleasant and unpleasant thing God does are all for His great glory (Numbers 14:21-23) that the earth might fear Him from generations to generations.

Make Us Kings Like Other Nations (1 Samuel 8)

If a man would please God to His satisfaction then he must ignore the idea of other men to cling to God's proposal. If you would see from God's angle then you must not be swayed by what you see in your environment or better not to be blind by it. The Israelites asked to be given a king like the other nation, why would they have said that? It is because they were moved by what they see and blind to what God wanted them to see:

- The errors of man (the sons of Samuel, Sam. 8:1-5): this has made many Christians to backslide, they thought if the children of this certain man could do this then how can this person convict me? That is why the Bible says we should look unto Jesus the author and the finisher of our faith. When we always see Jesus in every situation and not the error of human being then we won't live in errors. That is why we need to keep our eyes only on God through His Word. Many Christians today put the blame of their backsliding on their pastors and spiritual leaders or some other ministers and co-workers in the ministry, they'll say, "It is because when I saw their children doing 'this or that' and unable to be corrected then I thought it will be wise for me also to indulge myself." The truth is no one can ever have a genuine excuse before God.

- According to their cry, they have compared themselves with other nations they were swayed by what they have seen with other nations; freedom of will, indulgence, etc. But the Lord wanted them to see very well if man should rule them, that was why God enlightened them about having man as their king, not that God will not give them a king but they went too early to ask for it, God knew they will request one day but He wanted them to come to Him humbly for it (Deut. 17:14-15), that He might give them the one who will yield to His law and fear God. The plan of God over Israel and through Israel to the whole world is by one person – Jesus Christ, which is why the Bible is Christocentric, and its history is centered on the tribe of Judah by which through the linage Christ was given birth, which means that Jehovah God has purposed Judah as the kingship tribe (Gen. 49:10). The Israelite's thorough request made them to be given a king from the tribe of Benjamin, while God was preparing someone from the tribe of Judah. All what God said about the effect of having a human king all came to pass: for a few examples, God said in verses 11-17, that man as king will conscript able men to his service and as soldiers. And that eventually happened in 1 Sam. 14:52 which says, "When Saul saw any strong man, or any valiant man, he took him unto himself" Absalom also make fifty men to run before his chariot has God had forecasted; Naboth's vineyard was stolen by Jezebel; Solomon gave twenty cities to Hiram of Tyre, and so on all these are what the Lord had told them would happen. And that is also happening today amongst us the Christians; it's a good thing to have a mentor, but how are we closer to God? Do we listen to man [who can make mistake] more than how we listen to God who is perfect?

When man rules, he can never rule like God no matter how good he is, but when God rules, he rules like a God who is all-perfect; all powerful; all-wise and everywhere-present. Man is bond to make mistakes, God never make any.

Job's Ignorance

The Bible says all things work together for good unto those who love God and called according to His purpose, we ought to understand this always because some conditions are to be humbly required the reason from God Himself.

Job was ignorant about what he was passing through. He thought doing all those offerings and his righteousness can secure him, and so on, seeing himself in such a mess was a big blow on his face, and thus felt so disappointed, he was like "After all those offerings and righteous living!". He said in Job 3 vs. 25-26, *"For the thing which I greatly feared is come upon me, and that which I was afraid of is come unto me. I was not in safety, neither had I rest, neither was I quiet; yet trouble came"* And his friends also thought Job might have been sinning and that was why he was afflicted, but Job himself and his friend were ignorant about his case between God and Satan, even though his friends spoke some reasonable and preachable words, yet God still said concerning them in Job 38 that "they darken counsel by words without KNOWLEDGE", that is, they have spoken the right words into the wrong situation. I believe if he had patiently asked God first the reason of the affliction before blaming God, God would have given him some perception and he would have known some depths and where to wage war and I know his suffering will not be so complicated to him to the extent of him questioning God for what He didn't do. But after he had understood God and realized his foolishness, the Lord blessed him two folds of what he initially had.

Chapter 7

SEEING VANITY

Proverb 14:12; 16:25 says, *"There is a way that seems right unto man but the end thereof is death"*.

When man refuses to see from God's angle he may eventually be seeing from Satan's angle, and behold it is always pleasant at first sight, it is called The Lust Of Eyes, which usually attract the Lust Of Flesh and Pride Of Life. When we yield to Satan's proposal he'll make us see some beautiful distractions, pleasant snare, and sweet delusions, but behind it is a great pit. And thereafter starts dialogue — the first step to Satan's strategies; in the mind, that is why the Bible asks us to always flee from his appearance, because no matter how wise we think we are, Satan will always outsmart us. But when by grace we beat the devil's devise, we became stronger, but if we are defeated then we will have to start from the scratch. Now let's see how some eyes were open to vanity and how they are victimized.

Eve's Dialogue

I always tell people that it is not a day job for the serpent to approach Eve and to deceive her, it must have been coming and coming, the serpent may have told or showed Eve some interesting things that may have attracted her (as it is written that "The serpent was more subtle and [crafty] than any living creature of the field") before raising the topic about the tree of knowledge of good and evil; saying, "Yea hath God said, ye shall not eat of every tree of the garden?" Since Eve knew the command issued upon the tree she should not have entertained the subject concerning it, like I always say — you cannot dialogue with Satan and win it's either he lie as he usually does or tell you the half-truth which is even more dangerous than a blatant lie. The Bible asked us to rebuke him or to flee from his appearance, but unfortunately several believers make dialogue with Satan in their heart over sinful decision, they'll say, "Since that money is to help the needy then it is not a sin if you steal it"; and several people through it has made them to customize sin; they'll say, "That's a white lie", calling stealing borrowing, and so on, some will even back their evil plans up with Bible references. When Satan tempted Jesus, he used Bible references but the third time Jesus said, "Get thee behind me Satan." I believe if Jesus didn't rebuke Satan he would have kept on tempting Jesus because he never get tired of tempting; little wonder the Bible says rebuke the devil and he will flee.

But after their dialogue, the Bible says in Gen 3:6, *"When the woman saw* [even though she has been seeing the tree before but this time by what the serpent showed her] *that the tree was good for food* (lust of flesh)*, and it was pleasant to the eyes* (lust of eyes), *and a tree to be desired to make one wise* (pride of life), *and did eat and, and gave also unto her husband with her; and he did eat"* and that brought the world into what it is today, the lesson there is the more you dialogue with Satan the more you lose yourself to him.

Lot's Selfishness

Apparently Lot became rich by following Abraham, but thereafter he has no regard for Uncle Abraham, if it were not so he should have been the one to caution his herdsmen so well about the strife between them and his uncle's herdsmen, but when they decided to separate, the Bible says in Gen. 13:10 *"And Lot lifted up his eyes, and beheld* (lust of eyes) *all the plain of Jordan, that it was well watered* (lust of flesh)…*Even as the garden of the Lord* (pride of life)…." He quickly went for the fertile land beside a river. Of course Lot would know Sodom and Gomorrah was a wicked nation. When Satan established his show to you he will render your conscience weak that it will be difficult for you to admit the truth. At first Lot pitched his tent toward (and not inside) Sodom to signify that he was aware of what is going on in the city, which this present Christians does; they'll say I only befriend fornicator but I am not a fornicator, I only sit among the scornful but I am not a scorner, if you are the only rich amongst several poor people sooner you will think like them, this is the truth if you can't change them you part from them and if God did not send you to them it is better you don't mingle yourself with them. Sodom and Gomorrah was not a place to be but Lot disregarded it; he later dwells inside the city and there after he left with nothing saved his two daughters along with the spirit of Sodom and Gomorrah inside them which at the long run made them to lie with their father.

What causes war mostly among nations is this covetousness and selfishness which causes a lust for power. In those days those with power will want to possess every pleasant things they see that is not their possession even if someone has possessed it already, and it is been done up to now, even some so called Christians will want to covet their neighbor's properties that is not there possession. God himself do not overlook covetousness that is why He included it in His ten commandments to the Israelites. When Satan sights it in one's life then he'll capitalize on it and open one's eyes to see the [evil] benefits which can attracts so much but the end thereof is destruction.

David's Idleness

While David was having a nice rest on his house's roof when he supposed to go and coordinate an on-going battle the Bible says in 2 Samuel 11:2 *"And from the roof he saw a woman washing herself* (lust of eyes)*, and the woman was very beautiful to look upon* (lust of flesh)*...."* And later on David by his influence he killed Uriah to keep his pride as the king (pride of life). However the consequence was severe; his family became a disgrace and snare unto him: his first son Amnon committed an abominable sin with his half-sister, his other son rebel against him, slept with his wives and tended to kill him, as God has pronounced against Him in 2 Samuel 12:10.

Idleness is like a desolate land that after a while weeds start to grow on it till it becomes big bush and after a while all sort of animals creeps in. An idle mind is a purposeless mind; a heart without new vision, when a leader cannot think of new thing and been driven by the zeal of his followers he will eventually fall into errors. Sometimes it is called, "little sleep, little slumber" it makes the enemies to sow tares among the wheat.

Above are the three main things that cause eyes to open to vanity: dialogue with (or entertaining) devil, selfishness, and idleness.

Appointment with Abana and Pharpar (2 Kings 5:1-14)

This is an appointment with disappointment; this is totally a lust of eyes, an illusion of mind, a mirage of goodness, and a sweet delusion. Many young ladies want a God-fearing and a well-being man to marry, they thought they could identify a gentle man when they see one so they neglects the spiritual investigation. And most young-gent thought 'shining eyes' is the solution for having the right partner, and also many lust after beauty but eventually got bimbos, and many looked for good behavior but got pretender. The plan of God for everyone is always incomprehensible.

Naaman thought Abana and Pharpar were the best river in the region, but was prescribed a bath in the river Jordan. Also people thought young handsome looking pastors are only from God, and those ones that are financially challenged are fakes; a person that demands larger bills or gifts could offer solutions and those demanding for nothing are mediocre with nothing to offer. People don't want ugly process to solution; they don't want cross process to get the crown, or battle process to victory, but a sudden solution. Naaman thought Elisha will only strike the place and his leprosy will disappear but it's another plan entirely; a test for humility, obedience with faith and perseverance. But thank God he eventually obeyed and was healed. All that glitters are not gold. Many times glittering is just an attraction and it does not confirm things to be the best, and as a matter of fact precious stone does not come as precious to eyes until it passes through though processes. So brethren never compromise on things God recommends for you because they are always the best.

It May Start with Too Much Look

Ch. 23:31 says, *"Look not thou upon the wine when it is red, when it giveth his color in the cup, when it moveth itself aright. At the last it biteth like serpent, and stingeth like an adder."*

The reference above can be very silent in the Bible or too familiar with, but it passes across a great warning that can be easy to neglect. To look upon a wine to the extent of discovering how it gives out its color, and to be gotten carried away by it movements, then you might have definitely look it too much. Too much looking is very dangerous, it causes intimidation, fear and lust. The psalmist said, "Turn away my eyes from beholding vanity..." For a man as Jesus has elaborated, to undress a woman in his heart, then he has definitely overlooked her. Most things in this world are vanity: the beauty of woman, the wealth of the rich, the fame of the famous, the strength of the strong, the wisdom of the wise, but a man entangled himself with it when he is got carried away by his overlooks, but at the end it bites like a serpent and sting like an adder.

Ambition Without Vision

Getting ambitious without getting any vision is also seeing vanity — the lust of flesh, lust of eye and pride of life. Ambition is very dangerous if it gives no room for vision: ambition without vision is a pursuit without purpose. Many pursuit is based only on emotions and not reasoning; "My father who is a lawyer is a respected personality so I also want people to respect me, I have everything it takes to become one" but have never think and be ready for its challenges, neither think of how to be benefit to the society with that career which is the vision and the primary purpose.

Many ambitions today are not ordained from God, and it is purposeless, everything is just how to become rich and successful, but not what God is asking from you to fulfill.

Ambition often is a self-centered issue, but vision often is God's will. Jesus called His disciples out of their ambitions to fulfill a vision. Peter would have been the chairman of the Galilean Association of the Fishermen or being the best fishermen or consultant of the fisherman agencies, but when he followed Christ, God made him fisher of men, the overseer of the

'Sheep', an elder in the Apostolic mission, and eventually got his name written at the gate of pearl in Heaven, that is, he forsook the corruptible worldly honor for the incorruptible Heavenly honor. If Matthew was ambitious of how to get to level 2 in the government work, he would not have been one of the pioneers and an author of the Gospel. Elisha was not carried away by his rich family, but rather perceives the call and followed it immediately. David was not too ambitious despite all the blessed assurance of being a king, but he waited for his time he knew his dealings with Saul is not a carnal one, but a spiritual one as we have discussed in the previous chapter.

People who are too ambitious usually don't wait for their time; some cut corners, some don't even want to listen to the Holy Spirit again, they thought time is not on their side and disregard God's time, they always get anxious for nothing, they'll became jack of all trade but master of none.

But those with vision will always wait on God for fulfillment; they knew the race is not for the swift, so they sustained themselves on the vehicle of grace, they are not easily pushed toward a particular career because they have already seen where they are going and so they pressed on patiently to achieve the goal. Mike Bamiloye of Mount Zion Faith Ministry said he would have useless without the drama ministry. In his book, 'Walking Through The Fire', he revealed the challenges he experienced and despite that he never ceased to walk through it because he had a vision, he was not really ambitious about his life but carefully followed his vision, and now through drama his ministry is reaching out to the world today and will never cease. I have learnt through his life that in God's vision for your life you will receive a special 'manual' for the fulfillment of your destiny — his life blossomed on the platform of sacrifice. But an ambitious man will want to covet, even though he may never know the end-product of his ambition, just like the story of a pampered boy whose rich parent have a servant which must always oblige to their indulgence especially the boy, but one day it seems he cannot indulge the boy in what want he want at the moment, the boy kept disquieting until the mother responded, "I don't care. Just give him what he wants." But consequently the boy suffered a sting from a bee which was what he has been crying to have, as he cried pain to his mother, his mother was furious and tried to query the servant, but the servant answered and said, "It's not my fault; he got what he wanted." Likewise, many Christians today got themselves settling for less just because they were ambitious.

This is an ability to see and anticipate. Vision is always from God, who will not show you vanity.

Chapter 8

BLINDNESS AND SPIRITUAL CATARACT

The Bible says the eye is the light of the body when it is blinded then the whole body goes into darkness; confusion, perplexes, uncertainty, mystification, disorientation, bewilderment, lost, puzzlement and so on. Through this book you may have discovered what causes blindness, but in this chapter we shall be discussing about some major thing that causes cataract and spiritual blindness. In our world today these are the things that cause blindness:

1. Philosophy: This is beast that spit venom of blindness into the eyes of men, it transforms, it chameleonizes, it adapts; it fits into every idea of man but most of the time gets one lost, and a lost man is more-or-less a blind man. This is what the Bible calls the imagination that exalts itself against the knowledge of God (2 Cor. 10:5). This is a carnal wisdom which wrought an intensive reasoning as a result of curiosity in one's mind, and at the stake of that, one can disregard even some actual truth especially Bible's. For example, I have heard some people talked about the apple eaten by Adam and

Eve that it is not really an apple but a type of one particular sin, and some people try to bring evolution theory out of the Bible, and also I have heard someone say it wasn't Adam and Eve alone God created then but also some humans had being created but not in the garden of Eden and so on. These are the evil work of philosophy; they'll ask how can a man live six hundred years, how can the whole earth be covered with flood, and how can that great red sea be divided?. The Bible is forever true, all we need is to believe, and not trying to make diplomacy with some secular philosophical theories, because that is what happens when one handled the Bible in mystification. That is why the Bible as given us an adequate teaching concerning faith in the book of Hebrews; without it we cannot please God because lack of it causes double-mind for someone and thus making doubt in one's mind against the power of God.

Anyone who indulges himself in wisdom will end up in pit of philosophy. Solomon lust after it and he lost himself in it. He through the inspiration of God and his experiences wrote the book of Ecclesiastes for every lover of wisdom that they may according to his conclusion do everything in fear of God. This is saying that every reasoning and research out of the will and fear of God will be vanity.

2. Religion: This is another monster today that Satan has awakened to counter Christianity today. And this monster has sent the souls of men into darkness and people are being blinded by her doctrines and they have blinded people being their

leaders. Jesus Christ referred to the Pharisees (which are also religious leaders) as blind leaders of the blind people heading toward a ditch. Religion abuses the power of the Christian's Gospel by creating a replica of its authenticity; the belief in supreme being (as we believe in God), someone as the pioneer and or mediator (as we have Christ as the savior and the mediator), some books as guidance (as we have the Bible as the word of God), prayers, and some moral laws, and by these they believe they are the same as the Christianity and thus making it an ordinary matter not different from every other religion and thus making people to neglect it.

2 Cor. 4:3-4 says, *"But if our gospel is hid, it is hid to them that are lost: in whom the god of this world hath blinded the minds of them which believe not, lest the light of the glorious gospel of Christ, who is the image of God, should shine unto them."*

Christianity as Christ as given us is not a religion but a power to be the image of God; to be small gods (Psalm 82:6, John 1:12). Accepting Christ into our lives is what makes our eyes to be opened not some religion.

But many Christians who have their eyes opened still suffer from the spiritual cataract of which if not taking care of eventually makes one goes totally blind. Like the man in Mark 8:24 who saw men like trees walking.

What causes spiritual cataracts that cause blindness in Christian lives?

Negligence: Negligence is dangerous in the case of potential; this is the number one enemy of potential. When the Bible says, "Behold" or "Take heed" it is telling us to open up our heart unto these things that we can easily disregard, like some sins we don't really give regard to, some awareness that we easily wave away, some promises that we could forget after a long period of inactive. Children of God, what are people noticing in our lives, in what area have we being usually rebuked; either by the elder ones, the senior ones or most especially your younger ones.

For example, one day a girl was saying concerning her elder sister that she is very greedy over food, and covetous, I thought it was limited on food but the seed later manifested in her relationship; ending up in double relationship at the result the covetousness, though it started from covetousness over food but look at where it ended. Have you been noticing some little behavior which you think that cannot result in a bigger effect? It is better we see it now and take care of it. I could still see some born-again Christian that still do or say unedifying things that they see as only a minor thing, like for example, when you will hear them call another (normal) person a "mad". You hear some words and foul language that cannot edify another fellow Christian whenever they are provoked; usually in this century when driving or when disappointed when watching some sport games, and when arguing. Ephesians 4:29 says, *"Let no corrupt communication proceed out of your mouth, but that which is good to use of edifying, that it may minister grace unto the hearers"*

Negligence blinds, it creates self-centeredness in the heart of man, it hides the good potentials away from man and diverts it from fulfilling its purpose, and makes bad potential grow unnoticed until it becomes an uncontrollable size. Like the example given earlier in this book: a person who covets on little things like food and other material things may end up been dissatisfied with only one spouse and thus having extra marital affair and also greedy over monetary issues. A person who loves too much privacy may end up having an unnecessary hatred to neighbors and segregation, and we all know what the Bible says about hatred. Been too exuberant can lead to pride, for the Bible says be swift to hear but be slow to speak; been too forward cannot achieve such a thing. If it is easy for you to do something without taking permission from To Whom It May Concern then you are likely to be a trespasser of law or a robber. If it is easy for you to criticize and condemn then you are likely to be a rebel or hater — the holier-than-thou. If it is difficult for you to give audience to people then you may likely to be self-centered, or it is difficult to admit to mistakes then you are likely to be a tyrant, if you entertain argument too much then you are liable to arouse strife and of course causing riot, over inquisition leads to unbelief and possibly atheism, when you are always easily got carried away by a little pleasant thing you see then watch out against pleasure of life; promiscuity, seduction, etc. And so on.

Ego: This is when we think we are always right, and when we never admit our weaknesses, this is a silent pride. This is when you always exalt your own knowledge and disregards any other idea; it will just seem that you know better.

What I notice in our world generally today is that it is difficult to admit to errors, we will want to prove that we are eventually right even if it is clear that we are wrong, and this also is seen in the Christian world today, this is cataract. And also people don't entertain questions that seem to be controversial to their doctrines, and they see the questioner as an inverter or an oppositionist or an enemy or backslider. Ego creates self-righteousness and religious pride.

Ego has made people to turn Christianity into religion, it has wrought messianic complex into many preachers today that by following their doctrine alone only can make them have eternal life. But the Bible has given us the direct order to look unto Jesus the author and the finisher our faith. I have carefully notice that these days many preachers don't really preach the Bible but exhibiting their eloquence and how well they can interpret or teach the Bible.

And yet we still have Christians who have deliberately become blind; they are those who abhor those that are not following their doctrines (1 John 2:9), they are the hypocrites the 'holier-than-thous', they are the greedy, the lovers of money; their first priority in involving in the ministry is money, they are the slumbers who cannot spread more the gospel of Christ, feeling okay in their ministerial stagnancy; no new vision, no stimulation, neither inspiration. But all this are caused by one evil spirit: spirit of antichrist.

The Spirit of Antichrist

This is the spirit that silently fights the nature of God in us. It is a patient spirit that waits for time; it is a time bomb that clicks silently. It is a spirit of eventuality; it usually operates at the last hours of one's life (1 John 2:18), that is, it stimulates one to deny Christ at the end even after so many years in service (1 John 2:22), it reverses one's confession about Christ (I John 4:3), and thus making one a deceiver as a result of your story as a backslider (2 John 1:7). We all know that the Antichrist is coming after the rapture, which will oppose Christ greatly and blaspheme His name, but its spirit already has been unleashed unto the heart of many that it may starts its work there before he will finally come in its full form. It silently works with our potential; it develops silently the seeds we could not see as a potential danger. This is a spirit that blinds the children of God to know about their lives, it doesn't care if you strictly make yourself a man of integrity and always want to live in the spirit, in fact it makes everything seems okay; miracles still happens, no financial lack; more ministerial breakthroughs and success, more great teachings from the Bible interpretations and so on, but it anesthetic the pain of some slight error or some 'trivial' sins in our spirit. It never rushes to attack but it operates silently. This is a power that hides one's weaknesses and wrought new weakness into one's life making sin to give birth to sin like in the case of David and Uriah and Bathsheba, and when the spirit succeeds in one's life it clamps to finish it; the ministry, the legacy and the eternity like in the case of king Saul, it was the spirit that fought for Moses corpse in Jude 9.

I pray that the Lord will heal our cataract and restore our eyes, and every hidden weakness shall be revealed in Jesus name. And I pray that Lord shall purge our lives by fire and shall deliver our heart from the grip of darkness, even from the spirit of anti-Christ in the name of Jesus.

Chapter 9

SEEING GOD

Right from the ancient times in the Old Testament to this age there are many who have believed in God but not all has really encountered God; having much experience with Him. But those who have gotten one are able to do more exploits, doing things in an extra-ordinary way, and thus became out-standing among their contemporaries. Any man who will have a great quest before him will have himself go through God and God going through him; having an encounter, and this often have an everlasting effect in one's life.

The greatest encounter is seeing God Himself either through the spirit or open revelation. Seeing God transforms one from being an ordinary person into being an extra-ordinary person, because they have seen an extra-ordinary thing; it distinguishes someone in his generation, even out of his or her contemporaries that of the same ministry.

There are people in the Bible who have actually seen God (open vision and mostly in the spirit) and which has made their lives to be somehow special in their ministry.

Moses' Commission

When God commissioned a great quest unto Moses, He had to reveal Himself to Moses through the burning Bush at first to begin with him. Jethro only employed Moses as his herdsman since he was only an ordinary man without any job and married to his daughter but had no idea about his calling. Jethro may know little about the God of Israel (as he would have known about the gods of other nations) but never knew about God's dealings with Moses, and by the time Jethro revisited Moses after he had encountered God, he was amazed because of how God have used him, by then Jethro acknowledge the God of Israel like never before; he said in Exodus 18:11, *"NOW I know* (what it had never occurred to him before) *that the LORD* (Yahweh the God of Israel) *is greater than all gods* (even his own gods and those he might have knew)..." That is "today I believe even though I didn't really believe before". God encountered Moses at the burning bush at the Mount Sinai, sanctified and prepared him, and also gave him courage and an assurance needed through signs and wonders, and by that experienced he was able to start confidently and fulfill the first phase of the mission — taking them out from Egypt.

And thereafter he had to request for another encounter again for the second phase — to shepherd the Israelites through the wilderness, and this time he desired to see God. Moses said in Exodus 33:18 *"....I beseech thee, shew me thy glory"* Moses was so desperate that even after God had promised him to make His presence to follow the Israelite according to Moses' plea, yet Moses desired to see God one more time in another dimension; in His full appearance, in an open vision. God may appear to man in the spirit but not in an open vision and live, and that was why God had to cover his eyes that he may only see the backside only. And this happened at the beginning of their second journey into the promise land.

And by the time he would returned into the congregation after the encounter he had his face glorified that the people could not behold his eyes as before, he had become a different man, and so he could pass the law easily to them (the 'stiff-necked' congregation). And moreover it was easy for Moses to lead the congregation of Israel for forty years; he judged them, he counseled them, interceded for them, because he had gotten good strength from God for the task; he had never for once worn out or get wearied, he never got sick nor got stressed out because of the job throughout the forty years of the journey, his eyes was as bright as that of a new born child, and he eventually got a good successor ordained even by God for the rest of the task to compliment his work. That is what an encounter with God does; a ministry without God's encounter will be diminished in short time. But for a good strength spiritually and physically we really need an encounter with God.

Paul's Doctrine

Apostle Paul did not see Jesus during His earthly life; neither as he being under anybody for a special training or served under any Apostle who has walked with Jesus in His earthly life or any other person who had knew Christ before him. But yet he had being an outstanding apostle and a great evangelist of all time; he teaches as if he was with the writer of the Old Testament, he talked with authority even like Jesus, he possessed every gifts of the Holy Spirit and proved himself as the one with all the gifts of administration of Jesus Christ, his epistles are as if it was dropped raw and direct from heaven, that even some Apostles like Peter in Jerusalem apparently read it like a Holy Scripture to them also.

He was not afraid to die; it was extremely hard for him to retreat, he was a hard-core preacher, even despite every near-death challenges he had faced and infirmity in his body yet he still saw the proclamation of the Gospel as a do-or-die affair; in his word, he said (in 2 Cor. 11) *"...In labors more abundantly, I stripes above measures, in prisons more frequent, in death oft. Of the Jews five times received I forty stripes save one (i.e. thirty nine stripes) Thrice was I beaten with rods, once was I stoned, thrice I suffered shipwreck, a night and a day I have been in the deep; in journeying often, in perils of water, in perils of robbers, in perils by my own countrymen, in perils by the heathen, in perils in the city, in perils in the wilderness, in perils in the sea, in perils among false brethren; in weariness and painfulness, in watching often, in hunger and in thirst, in fasting often, in cold and nakedness"*

Why was it easy for him to do this, why is his Gospel so spectacular? 1 Cor. 12:2-4: *"I knew a man in Christ* (Paul talking about himself) *above fourteen years ago (whether in the body, I cannot tell; or whether out of the body I cannot tell; God knoweth;) such an one caught up to the third heaven. And I knew Such a man, (whether in the body, or out of the body, I cannot tell: God knoweth;). How he was caught up into paradise; and heard unspeakable words, which is not lawful for a man to utter."*

This was a great encounter Paul had. The Apostles had seen and talked with Jesus in His human body, but Paul actually saw and talked with Jesus clothed in His heavenly Glory, so Paul's words are directly from the King of Glory. He had had more things to say; more Gospel to preach, more instructions to give and more doctrines to teach, even from God, than any of his contemporary Gospels, even among the Apostles.

Galatians 1:11-18 says, *"But I certify you, brethren, that the gospel which was preached of me is not after man. For I neither received it of man, neither was I taught it, but by the revelation of Jesus Christ....but when it pleased God who separated me from my mother's womb and called me by His grace to revealed His son in me, that I might preach Him among heathen; immediately I coffered not with flesh and blood: neither went up to Jerusalem to them which were apostles before me; but I went to Arabia, and returned again unto Damascus, then after three years I went to see Peter, and abode with him fifteen days..."*

This in the above text has shown how he had become an outstanding amongst other preachers. He was made an apostle through that encounter (Rom. 9).

Isaiah the Messianic Prophecy

Isaiah started his ministry in the year when king Uzziah died, Isaiah wasn't the only prophet in his time his contemporaries includes: Amos, Hosea, Micah, they were all in the prophetic ministry before him but he was outstanding; his book is the first in the Bible amongst the prophets, and not only is that he is first amongst the major prophets but he is considered as the greatest amongst them all. Jesus said concerning John the Baptist that "Among them that are born of a woman there hath not risen a greater than John the Baptist..." only because he had being the one who first proclaimed the kingdom of God, and who prepared the way for the Messiah — Jesus, and so also that had contributed to the respect of Isaiah. Isaiah was known as the messianic prophet; he was who had made known more clearly the coming of the Messiah: His birth (Ch. 7 vs 13-14; 9 vs 6-7), His death (Ch.52 vs 13 - Ch. 53 vs 1-12) with purposes respectively, and in his book also has the words of John the Baptist which introduced Christ (Ch. 40 vs 3), and all these prophesies are authentic and accurate.

Isaiah 6 says, *"In the year king Uzziah died I saw also the Lord sitting upon a throne, high and lifted up, and train filled His temple"*

By the time he encountered God — seeing Him, he knew himself immediately and he was purified for his great ministry. Even though he started his ministry in that year, he may have being a religious man like any other Israelites, but by the time he saw God he became an extra-ordinary man above his contemporaries, became one of the greatest prophets, and his life was a blessing to Israel and to the kings in his time most especially Hezekiah. That is what when one sees God does, it distinguishes one out of many, be it amongst prophets or evangelists, pastors or teachers or apostles; your life will be a blessing for the nations.

Ezekiel as a Sign

When Ezekiel saw God he began to do things in an unusual way; he himself became a sign for Israel. Unlike other prophets, he prophesied in a hard and practical way; he was an actor and artist, he drew Jerusalem and its siege and also marked out route for the king of Babylon to enter, he laid on his left side for a year and twenty five days and on his right side for forty days just to give a message; he ate dung; he shaved his head and beard; Ezekiel demonstrated exile, digged through wall with his hands and acted this drama in the presence of the people and then used it as a message; and the most painful of it was the death of his wife, God said in Ezekiel 24:15-17, *"Son of man, behold, I take away from thee the desire of thine eyes with a stroke: yet neither shalt thou mourn nor weep, neither shalt thy tears run down. Forebear to cry, make no mourning for the dead, bind the tire of thine head upon thee, and put on thy shoes upon they feet, and cover not thy lips, and eat not the bread of men".*

And with all these he had never complained except for fact that he cannot afford to defile himself when God asked him to eat dung, but he never care about the repercussion, he always do as commanded (Ch. 12:7) without any shame but only focus only on the mission that it might be done. Any man who will do what he did in this era will be regarded as a mad man, even amongst the Christian brethren. But thank God for evangelical drama and film ministries whom He has raised for this end time in taking up Ezekiel's mission. But it got to a time that the people needed to ask him about those act he puts on that they might clearly understood him (24:19).

Ezekiel (who was actually a priest) was a very powerful tool for God in his time even in exile, not only for Israel but for other nations as well. God set him up as watchman for Israel and made him to be an intercessor, he was also used for positive sign also in the valley of the dry bones, he also gave a clip about the coming of Christ (21:27) and also the creation of Satan and his condemnation using king of Tyre's life as his type (chapter 28). The only priest in his generation that God chose to witness the measurement of the heavenly designed of the new temple and so on.

Daniel's Amazing Prophesies

By the time Daniel saw the Ancient of days, his vision began to upgrade, he turned from a national seer to an international prophet. Some of his prophesies correlates with that of John in the book Revelator. His prophesies was accurate the rising and falling of great kingdoms. Alexandra the Great, as he entered into the temple of Jerusalem, it was written that when he read about himself in the prophecies according to the book of Daniel about his conquest over Persia he was surprise that he even sacrificed to Jehovah. Benny Hinn in one of his shows he said when he'll want to prove to some people about the authenticity of the Bible he will take them to the book of Daniel to show the fulfillment of some prophesies. Even Jesus made references to his book concerning the destruction of Jerusalem (Dan. 9:27, Mt. 24:15). *"There is no historical record so complete, and none so concise and comprehensive, as that given by Daniel. No single writer has related so many circumstances, in such exact order of time, as Daniel foretold them. He, even in prophesy, is more perfect than any single historical account — Greek, Roman or Jewish.... [it] stands as powerful evidence for the genuineness of the Bible..."* By Wayne Jackson

Little wonder he was also regarded as one of the Major Prophets

Come up higher!

The more you go up higher the more you see. God asked Apostle John to come up higher; above his normal state to a supernatural state and at that process he was able to see more, than his counterpart or contemporaries and at the process he was given a powerful Prophetic ministry. Out of the Apostles of Jesus Christ he was singled out for a special purpose, he saw in saw in full details what no man, be it any past prophets, be it any apostles, didn't see or they might have saw a little clip of it but not in full, just because he went up higher. He went up higher and he saw God in His Glorious Throne, he went up higher and he saw the number of angels no one has ever seen before, he went up higher and he saw the past; how the plan for the salvation of man began, how the Lamb had released Himself even from the eternity past — from the foundation of the world for the salvation of man and the victory in heaven over Satan. He went up higher and saw the future events; the tribulation, the reality of the rapture theory, the Great tribulation, the judgement, the end of the world, and the both millennial and the everlasting Reign. In his going up higher he saw eternal hope, everlasting peace and unspeakable joy in practical — the kingdom of heaven herself.

What am I really saying in a nutshell is that those people we discussed above who had seen God in His Glory had seen something unique and thus they were unique in their generations. Seeing God gave them a special purpose and those purposes were type which makes a man to be excellent in his generation.

The day a man's eyes open to see God, the day he opens his eyes to see Jesus on His throne, his life will inevitably change for the best, he will be extra-ordinary to do extra-ordinaries, he will have to succeed in his generation more than his contemporaries as we have discussed above. When you are higher than your contemporaries you cover larger perimeter, they will have to seek you for help when their strength is limited, you will keep going when they are confused, where vision ceases, your eyes open even more.

The interesting thing is that God has never ended His relationship with man as that of old, neither reduced it, He is still interested in speaking to us face to face like Moses, He is still interested in showing us the things of heaven, He is still interested in showing us things to come, He is still interested in opening our hears to receive new things through His words, He is still interested in giving us power to do even greater exploits more than they before us. The question is are we ready? To go up higher from being a nominal Christian to a genuine Christian, from being carnal all the time to be in the spirit, are we ready at any time for any call from God despite the circumstances and ready to pay the price, is our heart pure, do we still doubt or double minded, are we still dominated by flesh, is unbelief still roams in our heart, are we still depressed and worried about situations even that which God has already taken care of, are we striving to go up higher over these things?

2 Chron. 16:9 says, *"The eyes of the Lord* [still, persistently] *run to and fro throughout the whole earth, to shew Himself strong in the behalf of them whose heart is perfect towards Him..."*

The Open Heaven

Brethren, however, we may not be given grace to see God as that of those we have discussed above, seeing God may not be necessary an open or closed [spiritual] vision but yet also in spiritual perspective and a deep study and enlightenment in our minds, when the Bible utter the word "Behold" then there should be a thorough follow through, with faith and a heart of obedience.

There are mediums God has created to reveal Himself to us, all what we need to pray for is the Open heaven. While doing Church Growth, we were taught about three doors which must be opened unto us in the ministry: door of heaven, door of utterance, and door of faith.

When heaven opens upon you, then you will see its contents. The Bible says a man receive nothing, except it be given him from heaven: be it vision, revelation, purpose, goal, task, mission, every secret one needs to know; for success, for breakthrough and so on.

When there is an open heaven, your eyes will be opened:

- Through his word: Sometime when teachers of the word of God interprets the Bible while teaching it gets me amazed and I'll think am I not reading this same Bible they are reading because of some wonderful teaching and enlightenment they establishes out of the Bible. Many times whenever there is open heaven during your mediation in the word of God you'll get your eyes open to it and there at that very moment you'll see new things that have not even occur even to anyone, in there you'll find some awesome revelation about God, solutions, acute understanding; wisdom and knowledge will be imparted to the extent that you'll want to explain to people because deeper things will be revealed, therein is the knowledge about our individual ministry. A brother while sharing about his ministry with me said, he had a dream where he saw himself in a large room filled with files, he said there he realized that there are so many undisclosed messages in heaven that people are yet to receive and out of them he was given only one in order to build his ministry on it. Heaven is still yet to release millions of revelations through the word of God onto people, but when there is a closed heaven then there will be no showers of revelation.

When our spiritual eyes is open to the Word we will be sanctified and be increased, our mind will be connected to God through our spirit and that moment you will feel the presence of the Holy Ghost there with you, and you will know more about God; his capabilities that one is yet to imagine.

- Through Songs (Psalm): We got in our hymn handout songs that were written many decades ago and still relevant and remained ever-green to our ears because of those great lyrics and tunes. Those great songs were written under an opened heaven, and therefore they cause open heaven and make one to be moved and closer to God. Those people God used for those songs, many of them pass through tough moments in their lives; some of them lost his family in the mission work, some of them lived as pauper, some of them lived as a less privilege and so on, but they seems to ignore all those challenges and embrace the grace of God for their lives and thus they shared it in their compositions and it (always) meet the needs of we the believers. And how was it easy for them, it's simply because they operated under an open heaven whereby they could not see their afflictions but only heaven which overwhelmed them and so what the heaven instructed them only is what they will consent to and not to the rages of storm and their tribulations unlike Peter, they got their eyes fixed only to the savior. That is why you have heard them say:

* *"When peace like the river attendeth my way, when sorrows like sea billows rows, whatever my lot thou art thought me to say it is well with my soul."*

* *"Someday my earthly house will fall, I cannot tell how soon t'will be but this I know my All in All has now a place in heaven for me. And I shall see Him face to face and tell them story saved by grace"* and so on...They knew could felt the angels and the saints praising God not really for what He had done but for whom He is, and that's why you hear them saying:

* *"All hail the power of Jesus name, let the angel prostrate fall, bring forth the royal diadem and crown Him Lord of Lords."*

* *"Then sings my soul how, my savior God to thee, how great thou art."*

Many great songs with great messages that cannot be controverted have they left behind for every believer to touch and see God. But God will have mercy upon us because these days, it is like we are basically looking for money or fame, because many amongst the songs we composed these days lack inspirations. And today we only sing praises to God mainly because He might have done something good for us. But when there is open heaven you'll see what God is worth in lives, and as gracious in every situation and your songs will become a sweet and wonderful Psalms to the ears of the listeners.

- In Prayers: Many prayers are powerless just because heaven is closed upon them. During prayer sessions we need heavens to be opened because by that we can be connect to God. This not always because of our sins, but also it may also be that God wants us to understand we are praying amiss according to James 4:3, and also be the territorial forces of darkness hovering over us and so we need to clear them off, or it may be that God is just silent at that moment. But we need open heaven upon our prayers: by then we will see clearly where to direct our prayers to; our minds will be opened, secret will be leaked, key from heaven will be given out, we will know the kind of prayer to pray, weariness will vanish and strength will be given, and whatsoever we decree will be established.

When heaven opens upon our ministry, you will never lack the divine providence even in the time of drought, things will got clearer to you ever than before, you will not be moved by the sight of discouragement the environment is showing, there will be clarity of goal that is the area of our calling, and most importantly you will hear from God on your daily basis; the Holy Spirit will descend, and possibly you will see God just like Ezekiel, because of course heaven opens first before seeing God. There will be showers of blessings, abundant rain, troubles will stop and strife will cease and there will an abundant hope because we will see what awaits us.

Romans 8:18 says, *"...For I reckon that the sufferings of this present time are not worthy to be compared with the glory which shall be revealed in us."*

Seeing brings reckoning, and reckoning brings persuasions of a good hope, and that is why Paul says in 1 Tim. 1:12 "I know whom I believeth and I am persuaded that He is able to keep that which I have committed unto Him against that day". That is, he wasn't ashamed of that Gospel which was committed into his hands and not afraid of man who to deliver it to, because he knew the world was nothing too be compared to the place his savior had prepared for him because he had seen its contents. And so anyone whose eyes is open will be heavenly conscious and will not be lost in this world as we have many Christians today who has today.

I pray that our heavens shall open from today hence forth, in Jesus name.

The Rented Veil

Since the death of Christ, the opportunity to be closer to God is been given to us, the will of God really is everyone should know him personally and not from the one admonitions to the other. He desires us to be always be in intimacy with Him. He said, in the book of Jeremiah 31:34 that there will be no need for chasing to catch people to follow God's precept, but instead people will just gather to share His greatness, even before you could say, "thus saith the Lord" few people will be there to witness and to sanction it because they will not be ignorant about it.

1 John 2:27 says, *"But the anointing which ye have received of Him abideth in you, and ye need not that any man teach you: but as the same anointing teacheth you all things, and is truth, and is no lie, and even as it hath taught you, ye shall abide in him."*

That is, we are expected not to be a myopic minded Christian that is easily swayed away by some catchy interpretation of the Bible, but instead he will want to be like those Berean Christian that even they might have been hearing about him did not care about the personality of Paul the apostle, but had to go back that they may confirm the truth regarding Paul's proposal.

The rented veil was part of process by which God want us to see by ourselves, and not to be ignorant to what any person will be claiming to be the final and uncontroversial doctrine. Many Christians today are still yet to look through the veil; they are still standing outside that they might receive from the priest, they still have the vail of Moses upon their hearts; there's no individual interpretation from the Holy Spirit but only that of the "Most Venerable Apostle" and no personal search.

Sometimes when I study and verify about some preacher's interpretations of the Bible that has seemed to thrilled some people, I would just see that many people are just been driven by their emotions rather than reasoning toward that particular preacher; they refuse to search personally and what their "Most

Superintendent Reverend" says is final, and that has caused ignorance and conflict amongst Christians today. But thank God our greatest treasure — the Bible has been interpreted to almost every language so that no one will be cheated and be deprived the truth he deserves to know.

It is God's desire for us to open our eyes to see beyond the first curtain and through the second curtain, because He Himself was the one who had rented into two the veil of the Holy of Holies of the temple that our communion with him may be direct and smooth.

Of course God has set some people apart to be the leaders of His church and been given gifts for the administration, but we ourselves need to know God personally more than how they have described Him for us.

Chapter 10

OPEN EYES: A MUST IN THIS AGE

Dear reader, in this age it is a necessity that our eyes as a Christian should be opened because we are in the age where many assignment is been carried out to abuse or defile our sprit man, they capture the conscious mind that our body may be bewitched by the spiritual forces.

Subliminal Message

This is a world where it is no longer new that subliminal messages as become the order of the day; such as sub visual or flash messages in movies and adverts, sub audible messages: which is low volume audio cues usually put in loud music such as metal music most especially, and back-masking, that is an audio message that sounds clear and normal like any other music but gives another kind of a secret message when reversing music. And all these methods of mind slavery are being spread out to influence people's mind to do things. When surveying the internet for more details about this subliminal message (of which I put to you also to do so for more information even if yet to know about it) I learnt that many cartoons have hidden messages even Walt Disney's, and many children are been caged spiritually, this may not surface quickly until they reach certain age and they will suddenly be difficult to control. And that is why yesterday innocent children are now today's perverts. Also I have seen many signs on postal boards, on the street, supermarkets and so on, filled with subliminal messages which most of the times portray the word "sex" or give reference to it. Many toys and pictures on stuffs that should belongs to kids are full of it, foods and beverages advert postal are not left behind, and thus therefore (sexual most especially) immoralities as become the order of the day. And even to my surprise the September 11 terror in the US was foretold in the dollar bill, the Seychelles rupees has the word "sex" in their fifty rupees, only God knows what hidden messages will be in other nation's money bill or so, only God could save us.

Now concerning this subliminal message, we also have gotten people who are skeptical about it, and of course every truth has its own skepticism. But the question I would ask is, if the subliminal message is not effective to the extent of controlling people's behavior then why are they being used more often like I have said many music and advert pictures are filled with it, and most especially used by the occult and in some companies also to summon people's mind that they may patronize them, and why would it be banned in some countries like the US and Canada.

The Bible says the children of the darkness are wiser than the children of light, but we cannot remained foolish to them, we cannot afford to turn the side of negligence to this things, our eyes should be open, our mind should be enlightened.

We cannot allow those things to affect us especially children because they are most vulnerable, unwanted pregnancies, rapes, homosexuality, drug addictions and so on are rampant amongst youth. Subliminal messages are so hidden to the eyes in sight or ear in sound in our everyday life, which it is difficult to be found even if you are looking for it. But while wondering how those hidden messages are being revealed, I needed to conclude that those people who God has used to unearth those secrets are those whom their eyes is opened

What could corrupt we Christians are around us as that of those subliminal messages, many books have wrought occultism and cunningness and ungodly mentality in many people's mind. We cannot afford to be ignorant to them therefore we need our spiritual eyes to be open that we may know the device of the devil against us.

Eyes Like Elijah's

This is a kind of eyes a man of God should desire; this is an eye that nothing can hide from be it physical or spiritual, what is hidden to ordinary man will be like a 100 inches flat screen to him. It sees conspiracies; in the darkest room, in the heavens, on earth and under the earth, in the firmaments, in the waters and so on, and as they are going on you perceived it. Elisha in his earthly life, could see almost everything and nothing was hidden from him.

The children of the prince of this world always go invincible during their evil operations, and we are to perceive in our spirit or see them. Man in one of the northern states of Nigeria when he will start his wicked operation he will become invincible, but one day he went into the house of one particular missionary, but on getting there immediately the missionary saw him and said to him, "Come here I want to talk to you." The man became frightened of the power of that pastor since no one has ever seen him with his invisible girded on before, so he had to run away. The next day, he came back to the Pastor's house with his girdle again in reinforced with more power, but yet again the Pastor said, "Come I want to tell you about Jesus Christ Power". The invincible man did not have any other choice than to give his life to Christ, and that is one of the advantages of an opened eye of a child of God. There many cases like that even in the church of God, for example, when God is saying out of the midst of my people are wicked persons, we are to know that we cannot overrule the fact that we have satanic agents in the church of God, regardless of how hot you may think the meeting may be, they will still want to try you.

A man of God went to a woman during a normal service and told her to stop walking upside down; to everyone else they are seeing an upright walk by the woman, but the woman said, "Yes sir, I won't do that again way," and by the respond it then became clear to the rest of the people that she was actually walking upside down. Many are giants, many are two headed, many are with horns, many are goat legged, and so on. That is why as a leader in the church we will need to be in the spirit as the Bible instructs us. Apart from satanic agents, there are also people who create strife in the church of God, gossipers, talebearers, rebels and hypocrites; they are those people who work for devil against the church, apart from being among pastors and ministers, they are in those departments we cannot even expect that such thing could come from; in the usher, children teacher, and so on, they silently divide the church and cause rebellion. That is why the eyes like Elisha's is most needed, because we need to see them all so that we will not fall into their snare.

Wake Up!

Christians in this century should wake up and not to be ignorant. Since we cannot evict ourselves from this world then we will need to be wiser. 70% everyday life activities are filled with evil, and 60% of it is against the children of God as I have emphasis at the beginning of this book. The Bible made a silent warning in Eph. 5:16, we should always redeem the time because every day is filled with evil. If God reveal the everyday plan of the enemies against we the children of God we will be amazed, but yet God took it on Himself to protect us irrespective of our negligence to warnings and signs: many doesn't pray on food anymore, the simple "I am covered with the blood of Jesus" is far from our mouth, and yet the devil do not rest neither gets wearied because of us.

Awakening is the proclamation of God unto His people. When we are awakened the devil will never cheat us, when our eyes are open we will never fall into holes dug against our lives. Brethren, it is a painful thing to be blind.

How well do we believe in the word God, how well do we get acquainted to the Bible and follow it, how well do we ask the Holy Spirit some questions about our lives, how well do we pray, how well do we wait upon the Lord, how well do we try to apply a godly wisdom to every of our cases, how well do we try to live a holy life — a life of Christ, how well do we listen to God, and how well do we obey? Do we listen to man often, do we always get carried away by what we see and hear, does the fear of man supersedes the fear of God in us? Brethren there are many things we need to adjust in our lives that we might see clearly.

In Conclusion

The Bible says the Light of the Body is the eye, it is important to have eyes, but it is much more important to open it to see with it. Jesus healed many blind people in the Bible because He knew how important it is to see with that eyes; the Bible says in Matthew 20:34 when those blind men went to him for healing, that Jesu took compassion on them and touch their sight and immediately they received sight, and what happened after? They followed Him. The Blind Bartimaeus, as he was usually called then, knew his story will change forever and his name will cease to be known as the "Blind Bartimaeus" when he received his sight. He never asked for money but to received sight, and after his sight was given him by the Lord Jesus, his story changed forever. The man who was born blind from birth after he was healed by Jesus, he kept on shouting, "Once I was blind but now can see", all around the town that they had to take him to the Pharisees, but I was never afraid to keep shouting about the testimony of "Once I was blind but now I can see".

However, as the physical eyes is important so also the spiritual eyes is every much important as Christian, and as Jesus opens physical eyes He can also open spiritual eyes, as He pleases Him to open the physical eyes so also He desires to you to see spiritually. He wants us to see God, see ourselves and everything in our immediate environment, and not be ignorant to the devises of the devil.

Brethren, I am challenging you to let your eyes to be opened and start to see from today...

Prayers

Prayers for ourselves

- Let us give thanks to God for the privilege He gives us; as we have explained in about the renting of the vail that we might have a direct relationship with God. No more "wait behind, I will give you the instruction I have read from the holy book" but we have been given a free access to the Bible that we might discover ourselves the secret God had in stored for us.

- Let us thank God also because He has never lost any battle and He will never fail.
- Now let us God to give us power for sanctification that we may be set apart to be used mightily by God.
- Let us pray to God to give us the grace for stability in our faith that we may not compromise.
- Let us ask God for a clear vision of Him, that we may know Him more.

Let's say this:

- Oh Lord, let there be open heaven upon my life from today.
- Break my heaven of brass and my fallow ground of my ministry in the name of Jesus.
- Oh Lord open my eyes that I may see You through your word
- Every conspiracy of darkness over my life be abolished in the name of Jesus.
- Every dark table of the enemies over my life be consume by fire. It is written that our God whom we serve is a consuming fire.
- Every Balaam of my life receive blindness, in the name of Jesus.

- You the spirit of anti-christ assigned against my life be consumed by fire in the name of Jesus.
- From today, oh Lord, let your heavenly vision fill my eyes, in the name of Jesus.

Prayers for the families

- Let's thank God because family is a plan of God, and that God have a special purpose for every member in it.
- Let us ask God to nullify every petitions of Satan against the family; that the blood of Jesus will cleanse any filthiness that has been ignorantly done to the family by the past or presence mistakes of any member.
- Oh Lord, cleanse by your precious blood, every stain in the mind done by subliminal messages in the heart of the children.
- Oh Lord, destroy every seed of immoralities, sexual and drug addiction in the life of the children. And we nullify every strange behavior in their lives for the glory of God in Jesus name. As children are important to God so also are they important to Satan.
- Oh Lord, destroy the demon of homosexuality in the life of every children, be it youth or adolescent. In the name of Jesus.

I have heard a person say, "I thought homosexuality is something that is normal and it manifested from their childhood", but I replied and said to him that that is ignorant of him to say that, but it's actually demonic.

- Oh Lord, open our understandings, and give us wisdom for a good administration in the family.
- Make our family oh Lord, gift to the nations.
- Heal our family's infirmities, provide for the poor, be our shield and keep us under your wings, and let there be destiny fulfillments.

Prayers for the nations

- Let us thank God for He is the Prince of Peace; He is able to bring peace to the ranging storm.
- Give Him all the glory due to His holy Name.
- Thank God for the Holy Spirit's interventions over the nations.
- Let's ask God to forgive every sin of the land; corruptions, killings, stealing and so on.
- Let's ask for the precious Blood of Christ; the Blood that speaks better things than that of the blood of Abel to cleanse and heal our lands.
- Now let's say: Oh Lord, unfold the plans of the enemies against the Land.
- Oh Lord, disappoint and destroy the conspiracies of the evil ones, in the government, in the force, amongst the rich and destroy the demons of religion, in the Name of Jesus.

- Scatter the gatherings of those who are please with wars and disappoint their plans and purposes.
- Uproot any evil leader and plant the godly people that the destiny if the nation may be fulfilled.
- Help our leaders to know and to do what is right for their people.
- Oh Lord, intervene in the affairs of the nations that are suffering and that are in unpleasant situations; wars, hunger, hazards and so on.
- Let thy kingdom come oh Lord in the name of Jesus.

Prayers for the church of God

- Let us give thanks to God for His promises over the church that the gate of hell will not prevail over it.
- Let us give thanks to the Lord for many testimonies of the church that edifies.
- Let us give thanks to God for the purpose he has for the church, individually and collectively.
- Let us give thanks to God for His blessings over the church.
- Let us give thanks to God for the leaders His has put in place to lead and to shepherd them.
- And let us give thanks to God for the revival He His using the church for in this world.

- Let's say: oh Lord open the eyes of our heart that we may know more about Your will, that we may not disobey or be right in our own eyes.

- Oh Lord, let there be open heaven upon our ministries, for authority and for breakthrough.

- Let the every siege wicked be put to shame and let the petition of Satan be rendered null and void over the church of God in the Name of Jesus.

- Oh Lord, open the eyes of those who you have chosen as our leaders that they may not be like a blind leading blind people.

- Oh Lord, give our leaders the eyes like Elisha's to discern and detect every hidden agenda of the enemies.

- Give us strength to always withstand the trials, afflictions and temptations of the world, Satan and flesh.

- Oh LORD our GOD, let your name be always glorify, let your children be blessed, and let the devil be out to shame. In Jesus Name, Amen.

About the author

Oluwafemi O. Emmanuel is a practical young preacher, a teacher of the word of God and a Bible college student in Nigeria. He is a co-founder of The Gap Filler Prayer Ministry, a ministry specially established by God on the foundation of the promise according to the book of Isaiah 61:1-3, and thus it is strictly to intercede for everyone; the Christians to be strong in the Lord, and church that they may fulfill their destiny and that the gate of hell will not prevail over them, the unbelievers for salvation, and the double-minded for deliverance. His call and purpose of God for his life has made him to be an author and a kind of person who is ready to give every moment for the progress of the work of God especially in these last days, and to contribute in the last day revival.

About the Book

The book has been inspired by God to explain scripturally the will of God for an opened eye for knowledge and a spiritual understanding in the life of a Christian. It will help you look deeper into a situation which can be easy to neglect and thus may cause spiritual problems for a Christian. And more the message in this book is coupled with series of prayers. It is time to wake up from our slumber and be delivered from spiritual cataract and move forward.

The Man Whose Eyes Are Open

www.ingramcontent.com/pod-product-compliance
Lightning Source LLC
Chambersburg PA
CBHW070113080526
44586CB00013B/1276